AIDS in the 21st Century

What You Should Know

Michelle M. Houle

Enslow Publishers, Inc.

40 Industrial Road   PO Box 38
Box 398   Aldershot
Berkeley Heights, NJ 07922   Hants GU12 6BP
USA   UK

http://www.enslow.com

Library of Congress Cataloging-in-Publication Data

Houle, Michelle M.
    AIDS in the 21st century : what you should know / Michelle M.
Houle.
        v. cm. — (Issues in focus)
        Includes bibliographical references and index.
        Contents: The AIDS epidemic— The epidemic and the spread of
    AIDS today— A global issue— Education and awareness: Ryan
    White's story—Advocacy, roadblocks, debates, and what's being
    done — AIDS and the beginning of the 21st century.
    ISBN 0-7660-1690-0
        1. AIDS (Disease)—Juvenile literature. [1. AIDS (Disease)
    2. Diseases.] I. Title. II. Series: Issues in focus (Hillside, N.J.)
    RC606.65.H68 2003
    616.97'92—dc21
                                                    2002152066

Printed in the United States of America

10 9 8 7 6 5 4

To Our Readers: We have done our best to make sure all Internet
addresses in this book were active and appropriate when we went to
press. However, the author and the publisher have no control over and
assume no liability for the material available on those Internet sites or on
other Web sites they may link to. Any comments or suggestions can be
sent by e-mail to comments@enslow.com or to the address on the back
cover.

Illustration Credits: Corbis Images Royalty-Free, pp. 25, 95;
Corel Corp., pp. 41, 48; digital imagery copyright 1999
PhotoDisc, Inc., pp. 29, 86; EyeWire Images, p. 75; National
Institutes of Health, pp. 8, 65; National Library of Medicine, pp.
57, 71; RubberBall Productions, p. 16; U.S. Centers for Disease
Control, pp. 21, 61, 82, 93.

Cover Illustrations: Digital imagery copyright 1999 PhotoDisc,
Inc. (background); Hemera Technologies (inset).

Contents

1

The AIDS
Epidemic

La Toya Rodgers, age twelve, lives in Indiana with her great-aunt, whom she refers to as her mother. Like any other girl her age, she wants to get along with her classmates and fit in at school. She wants people to think that she is just like everyone else. But La Toya is very different from most girls her age, and she has been for her entire life. When she was six years old, her great-aunt sat her down and told her something very important: La Toya has AIDS.

La Toya's mother had AIDS when she was pregnant, and La Toya contracted the disease from her mother before she was born. Until she was six years old, however, she did not know that she was very different from other kids. She did not know much about her real mother, but her great-aunt took care of her, and La Toya loved her. La Toya's great-aunt knew that because La Toya was very young, it might be very difficult for her to understand what it meant to have AIDS, but she also knew that La Toya had to know the truth.

La Toya's great-aunt cares about her a great deal, and she decided to tell her about AIDS when she thought La Toya was ready. She told La Toya that she should ask her if she had any questions about the disease or about how to take care of herself. She also told La Toya that she should let her know right away if any of the kids in the neighborhood teased her or made fun of her because she had AIDS.

Trusting her great-aunt, La Toya started school like everyone else. She knew that she had a serious disease, but she did not really understand that people might treat her differently because of it. La Toya did not try to hide the fact that she had AIDS, but it was not always easy to face her classmates.

In the second grade, many of the teachers and students at La Toya's school knew that she had AIDS. This was the first time La Toya really noticed that people were treating her differently because of the illness. Although La Toya just wanted to be a normal kid, some of the children in her class would not sit near her or play with her. "They called me AIDS girl," she said. "I was sad and went home to ask my [great-aunt] why did this happen to me, why did kids do this to me."[1]

La Toya's great-aunt told her that she was just like the other kids except that she has a disease that means she has to take care of herself in a different way. La Toya believes that this is true. She said, "The only thing different about me is that I take 15 pills a day." Believing this does not always make it easier to get along with children her age, though, and La Toya has had to face questions that most kids her age never have to answer—such as whether she is going to die and whether people can get sick by being her friends. She has decided that the best way she can handle her disease is to be honest about it and to try to teach people about it. La Toya said, "I told the kids at school that you couldn't get AIDS from touching me or hugging me or being my friend."

La Toya has lived with AIDS her entire life. She understands the seriousness of the disease, but she does not let it overwhelm her. When kids in her class ask her if she is going to die, she tells them, "When it's my turn, my time will come."[2] La Toya does not see AIDS as a death sentence. She sees it as a challenge that she is going to live with for as long as she can.

The AIDS Epidemic

AIDS, or *acquired immunodeficiency syndrome*, is a disease that causes the failure of the immune system. The name of the disease describes what it is. "Acquired" means that it is a disease that a person gets from someone else. The disease is transmitted,

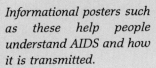
Informational posters such as these help people understand AIDS and how it is transmitted.

or spread, from person to person, and it is therefore a contagious disease. "Immunodeficiency" means that there is a deficiency—a defect or a problem—with the body's immune system, which is the system that prevents illness and helps people get better when they are sick. It is the immune system, for example, that helps a person fight off a cold or that keeps a person from getting the chicken pox over and over again. Finally, the word "syndrome" can be defined as a group of symptoms that occur together and that together indicate a certain problem. Thus, acquired immunodeficiency syndrome is like one "umbrella" disease made up of many symptoms or illnesses.

AIDS is caused by a virus called HIV, or *human*

immunodeficiency virus—a virus that affects the immune system in humans. Once it is in the body, this virus attacks and destroys healthy cells that help the immune system. There is a difference between HIV and AIDS. A person has AIDS when his or her immune system has been damaged so severely by HIV that it can no longer ward off infections. As the disease progresses, people with HIV/AIDS get more and more *opportunistic infections*, or infections that their bodies would usually be able to fight off. These are the symptoms that make up the AIDS "umbrella." Eventually, people with AIDS die of one or more of these opportunistic infections. It is therefore inaccurate to say that someone has died of AIDS. AIDS does not kill people. People die of diseases they get because they have AIDS.

Many people in the United States are beginning to believe that the AIDS epidemic is under control, but this is not true. Worldwide, there are about 42 million people living with HIV and AIDS, and approximately 5 million adults and children were newly infected with HIV during the year 2002 alone. About 800,000, or one out of six, of these new infections were in people under the age of fifteen.[3] These numbers mean that about 14,000 people are newly infected with HIV every day, and the numbers could get worse before they get better. Even though doctors and researchers are discovering new ways to treat HIV and AIDS, there is still no cure and no vaccine, or preventative medicine, to stop the epidemic. Throughout the world, approximately 3 million people died of AIDS-related causes during the year 2002.[4]

Although many Americans understand how HIV and AIDS can be prevented, the AIDS epidemic is still very serious in the United States, and it is hitting certain communities harder than others. Studies have shown that about 40,000 Americans contract HIV each year. Although there are more men than women with HIV and AIDS in the United States, almost a third of new HIV cases are in women.[5] Adults are not the only ones in America who are becoming infected—one out of every four people with a new case of HIV in America is under the age of twenty.[6] Members of minority groups are also at risk. In the year 2002, more than half of the new HIV cases in America were among African Americans, and nearly a fifth of the new cases were among Hispanics.[7]

Some Opportunistic Infections

A few of the diseases or complexes that commonly affect people with HIV or AIDS are severe diarrhea; wasting, or the rapid loss of weight; anemia; Kaposi's sarcoma; *Pneumocystis carinii* pneumonia; thrush or oral candidiasis, a fungal infection in the mucous membranes of the mouth; herpes; shingles; tuberculosis; and damage to the nervous system that may affect a person's memory or cause dementia, a loss of intellectual abilities. Many different kinds of cancer are also common. Women are also at risk for serious gynecological infections.

These numbers are particularly alarming because African Americans and Hispanics make up a much smaller proportion of the overall American population. Thus, HIV/AIDS is having what is called a disproportionate effect on these groups.

AIDS Awareness

The HIV virus is contagious, but not in the same way as the chicken pox or a cold. It cannot be transmitted, or passed along, just by holding hands or by sharing a bench with someone. The virus is passed from person to person when they share bodily fluids such as blood, semen, vaginal fluids, or breast milk. Therefore, the virus is not passed on through casual contact, and its transmission can be prevented.

HIV and AIDS can be prevented, but people must understand how the disease is transmitted in order to stop the epidemic from spreading further than it has already. Unfortunately, in many parts of the world, the epidemic is spreading out of control. Some people do not have enough information about how the disease is transmitted, and sometimes the customs and traditions of an area make it difficult to stop the epidemic. In some areas, HIV and AIDS are threatening the political, social, and economic systems of entire countries. The epidemic is now an international crisis. Doctors, researchers, politicians, advocates, and the public must work together to keep the world from losing the battle with HIV and AIDS.

Understanding the causes and effects of HIV and

AIDS in the United States and in the rest of the world is one of the most important first steps toward stopping the spread of HIV. Like La Toya and other kids with and without HIV and AIDS, young people can help the world by teaching others about the disease and, by spreading the word of AIDS awareness and education, do their part to overcome the AIDS epidemic.

2

The Epidemic and the Spread of AIDS Today

In the very early 1980s, doctors were confronted with several mysteries— mysteries that unraveled to present a disease more baffling than any they had ever encountered before. This disease was so strange that it was several years before it even had a name. Once recognized, that name was soon known throughout the world as the plague of the twentieth century. Its path soon frightened, shocked, and bewildered people from all walks of life.

The story of this epidemic began in 1981 when doctors in New York City began to notice a strange outbreak of

13

Kaposi's sarcoma in young gay men. Kaposi's sarcoma, or KS, is a cancer of the walls of blood and lymphatic vessels. It is recognized by painless purple blotches on the skin that are usually less than an inch in diameter. When the disease is far advanced, it can attack internal organs such as the lungs or intestines, but this often is hard to detect.

Until the early 1980s, KS was a very rare disease in the United States, although it was relatively common in central Africa (with the AIDS epidemic, it is now the most common form of cancer there). Many American dermatologists would not have even recognized it. When KS did occur in the United States, it usually affected elderly men of Jewish or Mediterranean descent. Ordinarily, it was not very serious and was usually treated successfully.[1]

In 1981, KS began to be diagnosed among young men from all ethnic backgrounds; the only thing they had in common was the fact that they were gay. In these new cases, the disease was progressing so quickly that it was damaging the patients' internal organs. The doctors could not do anything to stop the progress of the disease in their patients.

At about the same time, doctors in San Francisco and Los Angeles began to notice that they were seeing more and more young gay men who were stricken with a form of pneumonia that was sometimes seen in patients undergoing chemotherapy (treatment with cancer medication). This kind of pneumonia is called *Pneumocystis carinii* pneumonia, or PCP, and it is hard to diagnose because the first symptoms seem very much like a severe flu. Before 1981, if someone had PCP, he or she usually had some other disease that had weakened the immune system. Although it can be treated, this kind of pneumonia was later recognized as the leading cause of death among people with AIDS.[2]

Doctors were surprised to discover that these new patients were not cancer patients but people with surprisingly weak immune systems in addition to rather unusual diseases. All of them had been healthy only months before visiting the doctors, and they did not seem to be at risk for any life-threatening diseases. Somehow their immune systems had become very weak and were growing weaker. There was nothing doctors could do to reverse the process. They could only try to help the patients fight off the diseases that were causing them to become sick.

Recognizing the Epidemic

At first, AIDS was seen only in young gay men, and so it was thought to be a disease that was somehow connected to homosexual behavior. Because many people had prejudices against people who were gay, there was a lot of controversy about AIDS from the very beginning. Some gay men who got sick found that their families and friends either rejected them or refused to acknowledge their illness because they disapproved of homosexuality. One man said, "In my family it's still taboo to talk about homosexuality. If anybody knows, they don't say anything. They feel it's against God's will for two men to be together."[3]

In the early 1980s, doctors began to notice a baffling new disease among gay men.

He had become sick but still could not turn to the people who were supposed to be closest to him.

At first the disease was called gay-related immune disease (GRID) or gay cancer. Doctors and researchers soon discovered, however, that AIDS was not a disease that affected gay men only. They realized that GRID was not only an inaccurate name, but it also made it harder to raise awareness about the disease and gather information from other members of the population.

Doctors and researchers quickly realized that they were facing a very serious epidemic. In the fall of 1982, the Centers for Disease Control and Prevention (CDC) first used the term "acquired immunodeficiency syndrome," or AIDS.[4] In the beginning, AIDS was defined as "a disease affecting persons under sixty years of age who had no other illness and were not undergoing any treatment that might depress their immune systems."[5] It was diagnosed when the patient showed signs of an opportunistic infection, a kind of infection that a healthy immune system can usually ward off but which can overwhelm a person whose immune system has been weakened.

Soon doctors noticed that while AIDS was ravaging the gay community, other people were also showing signs of infection. These included men and women who used intravenous drugs, or drugs that are injected right into the vein, and people who had received blood transfusions. As more and more facts came to light, doctors noticed that the disease was also appearing in women who had had sex with infected men and in babies born to infected mothers.

Research Begins

By 1982, AIDS had come to the attention of researchers, and the race was on to discover the cause of the disease and ways to stop the epidemic. The virus that causes AIDS was discovered by two separate teams of researchers, one led by Dr. Luc Montagnier at the Institut Pasteur in Paris and the other led by Dr. Robert Gallo at the National Cancer Institute in Bethesda, Maryland. At first, the researchers thought they had discovered two separate viruses. The groups named their discoveries LAV, or lymphadenopathy-associated virus, and HTLV-III, or human T-cell lympotropic virus III.

Both teams of researchers had found that AIDS is caused by a *retrovirus*, a kind of virus in which cells store genetic information. Once a retrovirus has attacked a cell, it changes the genetic makeup of the cell. The groups of researchers quickly realized that they were studying the same retrovirus. By 1986, the confusion that resulted in the various names for the virus came to an end when the medical community decided upon the name "human immun-odeficiency virus," or HIV. Montagnier and Gallo were called the codiscoverers of the virus.

What Are AIDS and HIV?

AIDS is a series of symptoms caused by a body's weakened immune system. The immune system is a network of tissues, organs, and bodily functions that help the body fight off the germs and bacteria that are all around us. The immune system helps a healthy body to locate harmful germs and bacteria and destroy them, making it possible for a person to stay well or to recover from an illness. Without the immune system, a simple cold could be life threatening.

In AIDS, the destruction of the immune system is caused by the retrovirus known as HIV. A person who has the virus that causes AIDS is said to be *HIV-positive*, or *seropositive*. The prefix *sero* comes from the same root as the word *serum*, and in this case, it refers to the part of the blood that is clear and separated from anything solid. This is called the blood serum. If someone is seropositive, that person's blood serum contains HIV antibodies, or chemicals developed by the immune system in reaction to the virus. The presence of these antibodies indicates that a person is infected with the virus. If a person does not have HIV, he or she is said to be *HIV-negative,* or *seronegative*.

HIV disrupts the immune system by attacking and destroying certain kinds of white blood cells that are usually called CD4 cells, T4 cells, or T-helper cells. The human body needs these cells in order to have a healthy immune system. When CD4 cells are destroyed, for example, the body is not able to fight off diseases. When CD4 cells are destroyed, germs that enter the body are not destroyed, and instead, they survive and multiply. Because HIV destroys the immune system, a person with the virus is unable to ward off diseases. This is part of the reason why people with HIV and AIDS contract unusual diseases like Kaposi's sarcoma and *Pneumocystis carinii* pneumonia.

Now that doctors and researchers know more about the disease, AIDS is defined as "a specific group of diseases or conditions which are indicative of severe immunosuppression related to infection with the human immunodeficiency virus (HIV)."[6] *Immunosuppression* means that the immune system has been interfered with, disturbed, or suppressed (kept down). Doctors now look to the number of CD4 cells per cubic millimeter of blood in a person's body to determine how far along a person is in terms of HIV infection.

How Is HIV Transmitted?

HIV cannot be transmitted by being in the same room with a person with the virus, by sitting next to someone in a car or bus, by talking to or working with someone with HIV, or by eating, studying, or playing with someone with HIV. One cannot get HIV by shaking hands with someone or even by hugging him or her.

HIV can only be transmitted through the exchange of bodily fluids, such as the blood, semen, vaginal secretions, or breast milk of an infected person. HIV infection can occur when someone engages in sexual activity with an HIV-positive person or receives a blood transfusion with contaminated blood. Infection can also occur when

Researchers, such as this lab technician photographed in 1988, looked for the cause of AIDS as well as ways to halt the disease. Two teams of researchers discovered the virus that causes AIDS.

an intravenous drug user shares a needle with an infected person. A woman may also pass HIV along to her child during pregnancy, during childbirth, or while breastfeeding. The virus has only been found in very low levels in urine, tears, and saliva, and transmission via these routes is very rare but possible.

The virus that causes AIDS is actually easy to destroy when it is outside the body. Because of this, it is actually much weaker than the common cold, which is easily transmitted from classmate to classmate or between family members. HIV cannot be transmitted through contact with an inanimate object; a person cannot contract HIV by touching a doorknob or subway pole that has been touched by an infected person. Outside the body, HIV dies quickly and can be killed easily by using regular soap and water, household bleach, the hydrogen peroxide found in many medicine cabinets, alcohol, cleaning sprays such as Lysol, the chlorine used in swimming pools, or even heat.[7] Those who live with people with HIV or AIDS do not need to take special precautions to protect themselves from contracting HIV except when dealing with contaminated bodily fluids.

Transmission of HIV Through Sexual Activity

One of the main ways that HIV is passed from person to person is through sexual activity, because the virus can pass into the body through the mucous membranes of the vagina, anus, urethra (the canal through which urine exits the body), or throat. HIV can be passed from one partner to another, whether they are both men, both women, or a man and a woman. Transmission of the disease can occur even if someone has intercourse with an infected person only once. The disease can also be transmitted through the direct contact of the mucous membrane with infected areas such as open sores and blisters.

In the United States, the AIDS epidemic was first noticed among gay men who engage in anal intercourse, or intercourse involving the insertion of the penis into another person's anus. The tissue in the rectum is very fragile and tears easily, especially during anal sex. Tears in the tissue in this area make it very easy for infected semen to enter the bloodstream. The prevalence of AIDS in the gay community in the United States stems from the spread of the disease through unprotected anal intercourse, and the disease had spread widely even before it was understood. Because members of the gay community have been so severely affected by the AIDS epidemic, they have often been the leaders in the fight against the disease.

A Gender-Neutral Disease

HIV can be transmitted through vaginal intercourse as well as through anal intercourse, and thus AIDS is a disease that affects both men and women. The virus is capable of passing through the mucous membranes of the woman's vagina and into her bloodstream. The presence of another sexually transmitted disease can increase the likelihood of HIV transmission because of open sores or blisters that might be caused by such an infection. In 2002, 50 percent of HIV-positive adults throughout the world were women, although the proportion in America was closer to 20 percent.[8] The rates of infection in American women are increasing rapidly, however, and doctors and activists (people who engage in direct action intended to achieve political or social goals) are particularly concerned with the rate of infection in poor women and in women of color.

Because AIDS was at first thought to be a disease that infected only gay men, women were not originally considered at risk for the disease. Doctors soon realized that their understanding of the disease was incomplete, but research about the effects of the disease on women has not been as in-depth as the research on the disease in men. Women, for example, suffer from most of the same opportunistic infections as men and often have many other AIDS-related conditions involving the genital area and the reproductive organs. Today, more and more research is being done to study the effects of HIV and AIDS on women.

Oral Sex

HIV can be spread through oral sex, although studies are less conclusive about the levels of risk associated with oral sex. Oral sex that involves the stimulation

A Word on Condoms

A condom is a latex, polyurethane, or lambskin sheath that is put over the penis while engaging in sexual activity. Using condoms during sexual intercourse or oral sex helps to protect against transmission of the virus, because they block the virus's passage into the body. Without a condom, the mucous membrane of the vagina or rectum is exposed to semen during ejaculation or from pre-ejaculatory fluid. Lambskin condoms are not effective in stopping the spread of HIV because they are porous, or full of holes through which liquids, such as semen, may pass.

Dental or oral dams—square pieces of thin latex that shield the mouth—may be used to prevent the spread of disease during oral sex.

A female condom is a protective latex or polyurethane sheath that fits into a woman's vagina during vaginal intercourse.

When used properly, all these devices can reduce the risk of transmission of disease. However, they may break or leak, so there is always an element of risk. Thus, there is no such thing as "safe sex," only "safer sex."

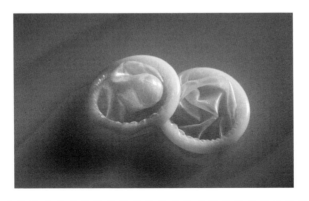

of the penis by a partner's mouth is called *fellatio*, and oral sex that involves the stimulation of the vaginal area or clitoris is called *cunnilingus*. There seems to be a relatively high level of risk of transmission of HIV if semen is ejaculated during fellatio or if the woman is menstruating during cunnilingus.[9]

Transmission Through Exposure to Contaminated Blood

A person may also contract HIV by receiving a transfusion of contaminated blood or by using contaminated blood products. Today, blood is always screened for HIV, and the risk of contracting HIV through a blood transfusion is very small. During the early days of the AIDS epidemic, however, blood banks did not screen blood for HIV because there were no tests available. As doctors and researchers began to learn more and more about the disease, they soon realized that they were faced with a serious problem in terms of the world's blood supply. As HIV and AIDS spread throughout the population, the amount of contaminated blood increased, putting more and more people at risk. Approximately 3 percent of AIDS cases were caused by blood transfusions occurring before 1985, when testing of the blood supply began.[10]

HIV has been known to be transmitted through whole blood, plasma, and blood clotting products such as Factor VIII, which is used by hemophiliacs. Doctors and researchers have not seen HIV transmitted through such blood products as immunoglobulin, albumin, plasma protein fraction, or the hepatitis B vaccine.[11]

There has never been any risk of contracting HIV while *donating* blood in the United States, because the needles used for donating blood are always sterile and are never reused. If people know that they have HIV or if they are concerned that they may have HIV, they should not donate blood. However, if people have not told anyone of their HIV status and they are pressured into donating blood during a company or school blood drive anyway, they may check a box on the blood donation form that says, "For research purposes only." This tells the blood bank that the person does not wish the blood to be used for transfusion into another person (although the blood is tested anyway). This option helps people avoid any discrimination associated with having HIV because it allows them to donate blood while keeping their HIV status private.

Transmission Through the Sharing of Needles

Doctors and researchers realized that AIDS was caused by a virus when heterosexuals using intravenous drugs began showing signs of the disease. When doctors saw intravenous drug users becoming infected with AIDS, they realized that it was possible for the disease to be transmitted through nonsexual activities. Intravenous drug users may inject heroin, cocaine, speed, or any other kind of drug right into a vein or into the skin. Drug users who share needles run the risk of being infected with HIV because used needles often have traces of blood on them. Drug users are also at risk of contracting severe opportunistic infections because drugs can damage the immune system. Because the immune system is being attacked on many sides, drug users may become ill very quickly.

One of the main controversies associated with intravenous drug use is needle sharing and needle exchange programs. If a person shares needles while injecting drugs, he or she is at risk of contracting HIV and of transmitting the disease to others. Although cleaning needles is not difficult, it may be time-consuming, and many people who are injecting drugs do not want to wait to clean their "works," as they are sometimes called. Needle exchange programs, in which drug users are given clean, unused needles, have been established in some communities to try to help fight the spread of disease. These programs are often severely criticized because opponents argue that they condone the use of illegal drugs. Community leaders often claim that the programs contribute to the drug problems in the area and that they only serve to fight one crisis by promoting another.

Advocates for needle exchange programs, on the other hand, see them as a means of helping drug addicts stay alive. Program supporters argue that drug addicts will continue to use drugs and share needles if they have no other options, regardless of the community's attempts to stop them from using drugs. Advocates believe that providing for clean needles is a necessary first step in helping drug users overcome their addiction and then stop using drugs.

Although there is much controversy over needle exchange programs, a study in the mid-1990s showed that the distribution of bleach (for use in cleaning needles) and needle exchange programs "can reduce the spread of the AIDS virus without increasing illegal drug use."[12] It is important to note that the study, which was conducted by the National Research Council and the Institute of Medicine, said that it was *possible* to reduce the spread of AIDS through these "harm reduction" tactics. The study did not say that these tactics actually did reduce the spread of the disease.

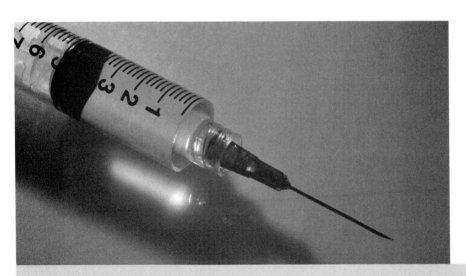

Users of intravenous drugs are at high risk for contracting HIV/AIDS. One controversial approach to this problem has been needle exchange programs, in which drug users are given new, clean needles in exchange for their used and potentially contaminated needles.

Transmission from Mother to Child

If a woman has contracted HIV and is pregnant, it is possible that she will pass the virus on to her child. This may happen during pregnancy, childbirth, or breastfeeding. Although breastfeeding is normally recommended for a variety of psychological and health reasons, women with HIV are often advised not to breast-feed if there is a safe alternative available, such as formula (bottle) feeding.

Throughout the world, there is significant controversy about the risk involved with breastfeeding. For many years, health organizations have been promoting breastfeeding over formula as the healthiest way to feed babies. With the AIDS epidemic, breastfeeding is no longer always safe. However, bottle feeding is not necessarily a good alternative, since in many developing countries, formula is not always available, affordable, or safe.

All children are born with some of the antibodies from their mothers' immune systems in their blood. Babies' own immune systems develop by the time they are a year old. All babies born to HIV-positive women therefore have HIV antibodies, but they do not always contract the virus itself. Some children born to women with HIV never contract the virus. Researchers are trying to determine what factors cause some children to be born with the virus and others to escape it.

There are some drugs and methods that can help reduce the chances that babies will contract the virus during childbirth. Unfortunately, although these children are healthy, they face serious challenges, because it is likely that one of their parents will die of AIDS-related causes sometime during their childhood.

The Battle Today

At the beginning of the AIDS epidemic, doctors and researchers believed that HIV entered the body and did not do much until it was triggered by some sort of catalyst, or something that causes a change. In the early 1990s, however, Dr. David Ho of the Aaron Diamond AIDS Research Center in New York City and other researchers discovered that the immune system began fighting against the infection from the moment it entered the body. Dr. Ho and his colleagues also discovered that this battle actually takes place in the lymph nodes, not in the blood. He believed that if there were some way to help the immune system fight the battle against the invading HIV cells at the very beginning of infection, the virus might be stopped or even eradicated. Dr. Ho suggested using a combination of drugs, which is often referred to as a "drug cocktail," to try to combat HIV in its early stages. Dr. Ho was in the beginning phases of a long research study, but even in 1996 it seemed that the idea of a drug cocktail might help people in the very early stages of infection.[13] Doctors and researchers are hard at work to improve these cocktails. Today, many people with HIV and AIDS use such drug cocktails and are healthier as a result. But they are not cured. These drugs simply slow the progress of the disease; they do not stop it.

Today there is treatment available for people with HIV and AIDS in wealthy countries such as the United States. With appropriate medical care, people are living long and productive lives despite their HIV status. Treatment, however, is not the same as a cure, and there are still many battles to be fought.

The fight against HIV and AIDS is indeed a life-threatening battle, and the comparisons to war are common—and frighteningly accurate. One man living with HIV said, "Not since World War II—which I remember as a kid, putting pins in a map of the world hanging in the kitchen—or Vietnam, have so many young people died all at once."[14]

Doctors and researchers, activists and politicians, healthy people and people living with HIV and AIDS, their families, friends, neighbors, and classmates—everyone has been fighting to come to terms with a powerful and seemingly relentless enemy since the first cases of AIDS were documented throughout the world. After two decades of war, the fight is far from over, but many important battles have been won. In the upcoming years, the world will face serious challenges as it tries to protect diverse populations from the disease and save countries that are being ravaged by its spread. It is a battle that must be fought from all sides, and it is only in this way that the world will destroy AIDS before its destruction becomes overwhelming.

3

A Global Issue

AIDS has had a serious impact on the United States, but its effect has also reached every corner of the world. According to the "AIDS Epidemic Update" from the United Nations Programme on HIV/AIDS (UNAIDS) and the World Health Organization (WHO), as of December 2002, there were 42 million people worldwide living with HIV or AIDS. Nearly 19.2 million of these, or 50 percent of the total 38.6 million adults, are women. Not all people living with HIV or AIDS are adults; unfortunately, a growing number of HIV and AIDS cases are in children. Approximately 3.2 million children under the age of fifteen have HIV or AIDS worldwide. More than 3 million people died of AIDS-related causes in 2002, including 610,000 children under the age of fifteen. About 15,000 of the total AIDS-related deaths occurred in North America—only a fraction of the deaths worldwide.[1] The widespread nature of the disease and its dramatic impact on certain populations has made the epidemic a priority for many world leaders. Activists, researchers, politicians, and the general public are all involved in the fight to stop the spread of the disease and save as many lives as possible.

Who Has HIV/AIDS?

In 2002, about 5 million people became infected with HIV. About 2 million of these new cases are among women, and 800,000 are among children under the age of fifteen.[2] While the AIDS epidemic is very serious in North America, where nearly 45,000 people became infected with the disease in 2002, less than one percent of the world's new HIV cases during 2002 were in North America. On the other hand, approximately 3.5 million people, or 70 percent of the total 5 million, became infected with the disease in sub-Saharan Africa during the year 2002.[3] This is one example of how entire continents are now facing huge crises as the disease ravages their populations.

While HIV/AIDS is a worldwide issue, the disease has hit certain areas harder than others. In some parts of the world, the epidemic has become a major crisis affecting the politics, economics, education, and the general culture of entire countries. The AIDS crisis in South Africa, for example, is changing the future of the country. One report has said that by the year 2010, South Africa will be almost one-fifth poorer than it would have been had the AIDS epidemic never occurred.[4]

HIV/AIDS in Africa

The spread of the epidemic in Africa has called attention to the interaction of political, economic,

Adults and children estimated to be living with HIV/AIDS as of the end of 2002

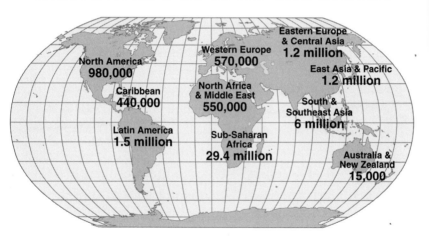

North America
980,000

Caribbean
440,000

Latin America
1.5 million

Western Europe
570,000

North Africa
& Middle East
550,000

Sub-Saharan
Africa
29.4 million

Eastern Europe
& Central Asia
1.2 million

East Asia & Pacific
1.2 million

South &
Southeast Asia
6 million

Australia &
New Zealand
15,000

Total: 42 million

Source: Joint United Nations Programme on HIV/AIDS (UNAIDS) and World Health Organization, "Aids Epidemic Update 2002," 2002.

and social factors that have overwhelmed Africa over the last few years and played a major role in the scourge of AIDS. Political crises, economic development, and the . . . growth of cities and means of transportation, as well as an increase in seasonal migrations between countries or regions, have favored the spread of the epidemic, which has become endemic [prevalent in the region].[5]

The HIV/AIDS epidemic has reached crisis levels in the countries in Africa below the Sahara Desert. This has been a region of crisis from the beginning of the epidemic, and it has been a particular problem because of its wide-reaching effect. No group of people has been able to escape the effects of the disease—adults and children, men and women, rich and poor have all suffered. With almost 29.5 million people living with the disease in this part of the African continent, whole countries are facing political and economic emergencies as their populations teeter on the brink of disaster. In 2002 alone, approximately 2.4 million people died of AIDS in this region. In some countries, more than 30 percent of the population has HIV or AIDS.[6]

Africa is a region that faces great challenges in part because of the conflicting influences of tradition and modernity and in part because of the many groups fighting for political and economic power. Education and health care are often inadequate or inconsistent within a given area. In addition, although many nations have stable political systems, others do not, and there is severe violence in some areas of the continent. Even without the AIDS epidemic, the future would be unclear for many countries.

The AIDS epidemic has also sometimes been spurred by unusual causes. In Botswana, a relatively prosperous country in Africa, more than a third of the country's adults are HIV-positive—the highest rate of infection in the world. Experts have suggested that the high rate of infection is due in part to the country's excellent highway system. Sexually active truck drivers have been able to travel easily from one part of the country to another, furthering the spread of the disease. This factor also contributes to the spread of HIV in countries such as India.[7]

Many experts argue that the AIDS epidemic in sub-Saharan Africa is due in part to the shaky political and economic status of the region. Unfortunately, the disease in turn often adds to the political and economic instability. According to the December 2001 UNAIDS/WHO report, AIDS is the greatest threat to the development of the continent. The report says the following:

> Most governments in sub-Saharan Africa depend on a small number of highly skilled personnel in important areas of public management and core social services. Badly affected countries are losing many of these valuable civil servants to AIDS. Essential services are being depleted at the same time as state institutions and resources come under greater strain and traditional safety nets disintegrate. In some countries, health-care systems are losing up to a quarter of their personnel to the epidemic. People at all income levels are vulnerable to these repercussions, but

those living in poverty are hit hardest. Meanwhile, the ability of the state to ensure law and order is being compromised, as the epidemic disrupts institutions such as the courts and the police. The risks of social unrest and even socio-political instability should not be underestimated.[8]

Theories on the Causes of the African Epidemic

Some researchers contend that the AIDS epidemic in sub-Saharan Africa has its roots in the area's cultural view of sexual relations. For example, it is socially tolerated for men in this region to have several sexual partners, and some men have several wives. In addition, over the past few decades, premarital and extramarital sex have become more socially accepted, but there has not been an increase in sex education at the same time. Health workers have found that it has been difficult to spread information about safer sex.[9]

Even with plenty of information about HIV/AIDS, its spread, and how to prevent it, sometimes social, cultural, and personal factors may prevent people from changing their behavior. In some parts of Africa, women do not have the same kind of equality as their American counterparts. Thus, young African women are particularly vulnerable; they do not often have the power to insist that their partners use condoms.

AIDS Awareness and Sex Education

Many people in sub-Saharan Africa do not have enough information about how they can practice safer sex, and there is often widespread suspicion about the use of condoms. Part of this suspicion is well founded. In South Africa, for example, the government was notorious for low standards of testing for its condoms, and many South Africans have had condoms break during use. In addition, many people have misconceptions about condoms. Some Africans believe that AIDS is caused by the condoms themselves, and still others believe that condoms are part of a cynical Western plot to stop Africans from having children.[10] Others believe that by using a condom they are telling their partners that they have been promiscuous, regardless of whether or not they have been sexually active in the past. These misconceptions are often ingrained in the minds of the population, despite efforts to show that condoms are necessary to stop the spread of the disease.

Most experts agree that one of the major causes of the epidemic in sub-Saharan Africa is the lack of information among the general population, especially among young women. In many areas, the majority of young women have never heard of AIDS or have serious misconceptions as to how the disease is transmitted.[11] Parents are often too uncomfortable to teach their children, especially their daughters, about sex or sexually transmitted diseases because these are considered inappropriate topics of discussion. Even if women have information about the disease and how it is transmitted, it is often difficult for them to stand up to their partners and insist that they use condoms. Many believe that their boyfriends or husbands will accuse them of sleeping with other men if they ask them to use condoms, even though most young women know that the men have other sexual partners.

Discrimination against people with HIV and AIDS remains very high in nearly all regions of Africa, despite the widespread nature of the disease. Afraid of the stigma attached to the disease and fearful of the medical effects, many people refuse to be tested even if they are aware of the availability of testing. In addition, many people who have tested positive do not tell anyone that they are infected, and in many areas, people often do not return to receive available treatment even after testing positive.[12]

Many people in this region do not believe that they will actually die from AIDS, and a relatively small proportion of the general public recognizes the seriousness of the epidemic. Many Africans believe that it is more likely that they will die from another disease, because of an accident, or in civil unrest. Many people do not believe that they will die slowly from a disease such as AIDS, and it is common for people to not see the significance of AIDS for themselves or their community.[13] Sometimes such immediate concerns as hunger, poverty, and war can overshadow concern about a slow death from AIDS. Studies have shown, however, that the disease is a serious danger to everyone in this region.

How Are Governments Involved?

Activists argue that the governments of some nations need to do more to stop the spread of the disease. For

In some parts of Africa, especially rural areas, people do not have access to up-to-date health care, including treatment for HIV/AIDS.

example, there is much debate about the official stance in South Africa, where the AIDS crisis has reached astronomical proportions. One report suggests that as many as 40 percent of all adult deaths in South Africa in the year 2000 were AIDS-related and that between 4 and 7 million people will die of the disease in the country over the next decade.[14] The government of South Africa has denied the impact of the disease, and it is argued that the president, Thabo Mbeki, perpetuates the denial.

It has been reported that Mbeki argues that HIV does not cause AIDS, despite the consensus of the scientific community. It has become "politically incorrect to talk about treating AIDS" in South Africa because this would suggest that HIV does in fact cause the disease, which the country's president does not believe.[15] Instead of HIV, Mbeki blames poverty, diet, and other social problems as the more likely causes of the epidemic.[16] He has also gone on record to argue that the powerful antiretroviral drugs used to combat the disease are "too toxic, too costly and are not proven to be effective," although many government officials use the drugs themselves.[17]

At this time, the South African government will not allow the use of many powerful AIDS drugs in state-run hospitals, despite studies that have shown their effectiveness. On the whole, the drugs are very difficult to obtain in most of the country, even in private hospitals. Recently, the relief agency Médecins Sans Frontières (Doctors Without Borders) announced a plan to import generic versions (versions not protected by patents or trademarks) of several AIDS medicines. The relief group plans to distribute the drugs to a small number of people with AIDS near Cape Town.[18]

The Availability of HIV and AIDS Medications

The availability of antiretroviral medications— medications that fight retroviruses such as HIV—is a significant issue in the effort to combat the AIDS epidemic in Africa and, indeed, in many low-income regions. In higher income countries such as the United State and France, doctors have seen very positive results from combinations of medications like AZT, a medicine that slows the replication of HIV, and various protease inhibitors, which Dr. David Ho discovered in the 1990s. It is important to note that these drugs may help people with HIV and AIDS, but they often have serious side effects. However, while people with AIDS still face severe medical difficulties and these drugs are not a cure, there is now hope that those with the disease can lead productive lives for a longer period of time with the help of medication.

Unfortunately, antiretroviral drugs are very expensive, and because of the wide-reaching spread of the disease in less developed countries, many of the neediest people do not have access to the drugs. Leaders in the fight against AIDS have called upon international pharmaceutical companies to join in the global fight against the spread of the disease by lowering prices. Some governments have called for huge increases in spending to help combat the disease. President George W. Bush, for example, proposed spending $500 million to help "save children from disease and death." Bush said, "Medical science gives us the power to save these young lives. Conscience demands we do so."[19] In addition, in his State of the Union address in January 2003, Bush pledged to ask Congress to increase funding to $15 billion over the next five years to fight AIDS in Africa and the Caribbean.[20]

The availability of medication has been a topic of debate throughout the world for the past decade and especially in the past several years. One of the issues that underlie the debate is the suggestion that the limited availability of drugs in poorer nations represents a racist action on the part of the West. Another argument is that greed on the part of politicians and big businesses is hampering attempts to stop the spread of disease. Pharmaceutical companies in turn argue that they simply cannot afford to supply whole countries with low-income or free medications or that the costs of doing so would raise prices in other areas of the world. They also argue against the production of generic versions of certain medications, saying that this infringes on the rights of the people who discovered these medications. On the other side, advocates for increased drug distribution in developing nations also recognize that the AIDS crisis will not be solved simply by dumping drugs on the problem. Health care systems need to be improved, people need to be educated, doctors need appropriate training, and tests for HIV need to be easier to administer and offered and marketed more widely.

Progress in Drug Distribution

Progress has been slow in the fight to bring antiretroviral medication to sub-Saharan Africa, but there have been some improvements in the area recently. By the end of 2001, more than ten African countries were offering antiretroviral treatment to people infected by HIV and AIDS, although not all of this is government funded. In Botswana, where nearly 39 percent of adults are HIV-positive, the government increased its spending and negotiated with international pharmaceutical companies for lower prices so that it could provide drugs through its public health system.[21] Some companies have also lowered prices, and production and distribution of generic drugs has increased in the area in general.

Fighting the Disease, With or Without Medication

HIV and AIDS have affected many people throughout the world, and because of this, the epidemic has been examined from many different cultural angles. Doctors and scientists have studied HIV and AIDS and have tried innumerable methods of ridding the world of the disease. Healers from all backgrounds have now had to tackle HIV and AIDS, but no one has discovered a cure.

Sometimes there is a conflict between traditional methods of combating the disease and the more modern, Western practices used to treat those with HIV and AIDS. However, many traditional remedies, such as powerful herbs, can interact negatively with the powerful antiretroviral drugs. Doctors sometimes have a hard time convincing patients that they should trust modern methods over those of traditional healers.[22]

The interaction of traditions does not have to be negative, however. In many African communities, for example, the sick often go to traditional healers before visiting hospital physicians. Today, these healers have become part of the effort to combat HIV and AIDS. Recognizing the respect traditional healers usually receive from the community at large, many state-run hospitals are inviting traditional healers to receive training about the disease. There, they learn about the need for latex gloves and the necessity of sterilizing needles used to inject medicine, among other things.

Further Challenges in Africa's Fight Against HIV and AIDS

Unfortunately, many of the people who die of AIDS in Africa are the main wage earners for their families. With their deaths, many families who are poor to begin with plummet further into poverty. Children, especially young girls, are often pulled out of school to help to take care of sick relatives or to earn money to feed their families. This in turn threatens the long-term development of the region, because these children rarely get to return to finish their education and the cycle of poverty and ignorance continues.

Young people in Africa are facing a very bleak future as HIV and AIDS ravage the continent. By the end of 2000, for example, more than 12.1 million African children had lost one or both parents to the disease. Experts believe that this number will more than double over the next decade. Additionally, in 1999 alone, approximately 860,000 children in sub-Saharan Africa lost their teachers to AIDS.[23] Despite the efforts to combat the disease through the spread of medical information and education about safer sex practices, the region will be hard-pressed to care for the generations of children left orphaned in the coming decades.

Has North Africa Been Spared?

The significant epidemic in Africa has centered on the areas below the Sahara Desert, but other areas have not been able to avoid the epidemic entirely. In the countries of North Africa and the Middle East, the spread of HIV and AIDS has been slow but steady. In North Africa, there were about 550,000 people living with HIV/AIDS by 2002. Activist groups around the world are worried that there are not adequate systems in place to stop the disease and treat those people who have been infected. In this region, the disease is mainly transmitted through sexual intercourse between men and women and by intravenous drug use. There are several groups of people, such as prisoners and intravenous drug

HIV/AIDS has had an enormous impact on Africa, even among those who are healthy. For instance, millions of children have lost their teachers to AIDS.

users, who are particularly vulnerable to the disease because of the lack of prevention programs and the political instability of the region.[24]

Eastern Europe and Central Asia

Though the AIDS epidemic has reached emergency levels in Africa, many other regions are also facing serious challenges. For example, in Eastern Europe and Central Asia, HIV infection is increasing at a rate faster than anywhere else in the world. In 2002 alone, there were 250,000 new cases of HIV in these areas, raising the total number of people living with HIV and AIDS to 1.2 million.[25]

In the countries of the former Soviet Union, the HIV/AIDS epidemic has been spurred by another serious crisis. In the last several years, there has been a marked increase in the number of young people using intravenous drugs. In this region, there are extremely high levels of unemployment and economic and social instability at the same time that public health services are deteriorating. More and more young people are turning to drugs, and drug use is becoming a significant part of youth culture in many areas. Many young people are not finishing school, and even those who remain in school face a culture in which drug use and needle sharing are common. Young people in this region are also becoming more sexually active without an increase in safer sex practices. All these factors have combined so that the HIV/AIDS epidemic is poised for an explosion.[26]

Fortunately, efforts to educate young people and

improve the economic climate of the region may help curb the spread of the disease. Experts suggest that significant efforts by governments can turn the tide, and several countries in the region have committed themselves to launching serious campaigns against HIV/AIDS.[27]

Western Europe

Western European countries saw the rise of the epidemic in the late 1970s and early 1980s, just as the United States did. At the end of 2002, approximately 570,000 people in Western Europe were living with HIV/AIDS, approximately 25 percent of them women. About 30,000 people were newly infected with HIV in the year 2002.[28] Treatment is available in countries in Western Europe, and while this has had positive results for many people, as in the United States, misconceptions about the spread of HIV and AIDS are returning. Many people in the general population believe that the epidemic is under control, despite efforts by government officials and activists to convince them otherwise, and this is leading them to engage in risky behavior. Thus, unless prevention efforts are redoubled and the general population re-educates itself, the HIV/AIDS epidemic could get significantly worse in Western Europe over the course of the next few years.

Asia and the Pacific

Until quite recently, only a few regions in Asia faced serious AIDS epidemics. However, now the disease is spreading throughout the region. As of 2002, there were 7.2 million adults and children living with HIV and AIDS in Asia. This includes people in Cambodia, Myanmar, Thailand, China, India, and Indonesia, among other countries. In 2002 alone, there were almost a million new cases of the disease in this region. This is a 10 percent increase in one year.[29] Intravenous drug users and sex workers are at particular risk, but there are suggestions that the general population is facing a serious crisis as well.

The region has had some success in controlling the spread of the disease, however. For example, AIDS was first identified in Thailand in 1984 among intravenous drug users. The epidemic spread to sex workers, then to heterosexual men, and then to women.[30] By the early 1990s, over 10 percent of young men living in the northern part of the country were infected.[31] Recognizing the seriousness of the problem, Thailand's government established a program to combat the disease, including a program to promote the use of condoms. In the early 1990s, approximately 140,000 people per year were infected with HIV. That number was down to approximately 30,000 in 2001. AIDS is still a significant problem in Thailand, but the program results show that there are ways to curb the spread of the disease.[32] Unfortunately, many countries in this region do not have well-funded prevention programs, and there are serious social and legal barriers that have made the disease difficult to combat.

Latin America and the Caribbean

In Latin America and the Caribbean, about 1.9 million adults and children have HIV. Approximately 210,000 of these were newly infected in 2002.[33] The disease has been seen in this area since the beginning of the worldwide epidemic. Haitian immigrants to the United States, for example, were among the first people in whom AIDS was seen.[34]

One country that is being recognized for its successes in fighting the AIDS epidemic is Brazil. Brazil has overhauled its health system in the past decade, and since 1997, nearly every AIDS patient in Brazil has been able to receive—free of charge—the same medications used by patients in wealthier countries.[35]

The spread of HIV in the Caribbean has had a significant impact on the spread of the epidemic globally. In this region, there are big differences between rich and poor, and many people move frequently from place to place. The tourist industry is also very significant in this region, so many people visit the area from other countries. These visitors often help to spread the disease in part because they may have unprotected sex with people who live in the area. In turn, some visitors return to their homelands carrying the disease.

Origins of the Global Epidemic

People throughout the world have asked how HIV and AIDS began and how the epidemic spread so quickly. Researchers have studied the origins of the disease, and there are many scientific theories about the epidemic—none of which have been proven. Outside the scientific community, there are a multitude of stories about the origin of HIV. These stories range from unproven allegations to almost mythic fairy tales.

In reality, there is no single person who began the AIDS epidemic, but the myths about the spread of the disease help to illustrate how small the world really is and how futile it is to try to determine who to blame. No country exists in a vacuum, and no continent has been able to escape this deadly disease. However, just as no single country can keep the disease from crossing its borders, no single country can stamp out the spread of the disease in the world on its own. It is only together that the world can eradicate HIV and AIDS and save future generations from its terrible consequences.

4

Education and Awareness

In the fall of 1985, Ryan White was thirteen years old and ready for the new school year to begin at Western Middle School in Kokomo, Indiana. Like many kids his age, he had a paper route and liked skateboarding and Mexican food. He had good friends in his neighborhood whom he had known since he was little, and he had a girlfriend named Kris. He was excited to go back to school to see his friends, and he just wanted to be a normal teenager like everyone else. But Ryan was not a normal teenager. He had AIDS, and Western Middle School did not want him to come back to school.

When Ryan was born in December 1971, his parents and doctors discovered that he was a hemophiliac, which meant that his blood did not clot regularly. If a hemophiliac gets a cut, he can bleed to death if he does not get treatment. Hemophilia is a hereditary disorder that usually only affects males. Ryan's doctors and parents were surprised that he had hemophilia because no one else in his family seemed to have the disorder, but the Whites did the best they could to help Ryan live a regular life.

Later, when he was older, Ryan used a product called Factor VIII, which many hemophiliacs use to help their blood clot. Doctors had discovered a way to extract Factor VIII from blood that other people donated, and hemophiliacs often receive injections of Factor VIII when they have a cut or "bleed" (internal bleeding). Unfortunately, if the blood from which Factor VIII was extracted was contaminated with HIV, all those who used the product were at risk of contracting HIV, although no one knew it was risky at the time. At some point, Ryan White received an injection of Factor VIII contaminated with HIV. He learned he had AIDS just after Christmas in 1984.[1]

Ignorance and Prejudice in the Community

After being sick for several months and missing nearly all of the previous school year, Ryan was well enough to return to school in August 1985, although he would have to start seventh grade over again. When his school told him he could not join his class-mates, Ryan was mad. Later he wrote, "It was bad enough that I had to start seventh grade all over again. Now I was being expelled for no reason."[2] Ryan's mom, Jeanne, and his younger sister, Andrea, knew how much it meant for him to go back to school, so the family decided to fight for Ryan's right to go to school.

Ryan soon made national news, and the small town of Kokomo seemed to be in the headlines every day. Parents in Kokomo were afraid to let their children go to school with Ryan because they thought their children could be infected by him. Even after they had been told how AIDS was transmitted, they still did not want to take any chances. Some of them did not believe that AIDS could not be transmitted through casual contact, and many kept asking, "What if . . . ?" AIDS was a relatively new disease, and many people were unwilling to trust what doctors and scientists said, because new information seemed to be coming out all the time.

Ryan and his family went to court to try to get the school to let him return, but it was a long and difficult fight. Suddenly it seemed as if the whole town was against them. People were constantly insulting Ryan, and the whole family was treated like outsiders even though they had lived there all their lives. Ryan and his family felt threatened at school, at the grocery store, and even at church. It was scary at times. Their house was robbed, and all their Christmas presents were stolen one night when the family was visiting Ryan in the hospital. Someone even shot a bullet through one of the windows in their house. Eventually, the discrimination was too much, and the Whites decided to move to the nearby town of Cicero, Indiana.

AIDS Education in the Classroom: A Success Story

In Cicero, the Whites met a very different community. Determined to help Ryan, the students and teachers at his new school spent a few weeks learning about AIDS before Ryan joined them. The students had the opportunity to ask as many

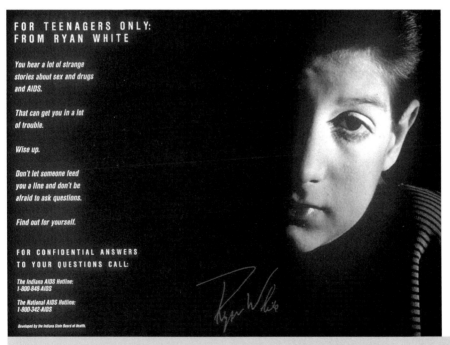

FOR TEENAGERS ONLY:
FROM RYAN WHITE

You hear a lot of strange
stories about sex and drugs
and AIDS.

That can get you in a lot
of trouble.

Wise up.

Don't let someone feed
you a line and don't be
afraid to ask questions.

Find out for yourself.

FOR CONFIDENTIAL ANSWERS
TO YOUR QUESTIONS CALL:

The Indiana AIDS Hotline:
1-800-848-AIDS

The National AIDS Hotline:
1-800-342-AIDS

Developed by the Indiana State Board of Health.

Ryan White contracted AIDS through contaminated blood. Though he faced ignorance and prejudice in his community, he became a powerful spokesman for AIDS awareness and education.

questions as they wanted, and when the teachers felt that the students were ready to welcome Ryan, the school went out into the community at large to educate them about the disease. Some parents were nervous about having their teenagers attend school with someone with AIDS, but, as Ryan wrote later,

> The school's idea of starting with the students worked. Kids told their parents they understood AIDS wasn't contagious [the way a cold is], they weren't scared of me, and they wanted to be in school. One family asked their kid to stay home, and the kid said no![3]

When Ryan finally entered his new school, he felt very welcome.

Ryan's story illustrates the importance of AIDS awareness and education. Although he had faced severe hardships in Kokomo, Ryan's fight eventually helped people with AIDS all over the world. He became an active speaker who called for AIDS education. He helped to educate students and teachers, met with entertainment and sports celebrities, and even spoke before the President's Commission on AIDS in 1989. After Ryan died in April 1990 at the age of eighteen, his quest for fair treatment for people with HIV and AIDS was not forgotten. In 1990, Congress passed the Ryan White Comprehensive AIDS Resources Emergency (CARE) Act, which helps communities provide financial assistance and other services to people with HIV and their families.

Who Has HIV and AIDS in the United States?

Doctors, researchers, government officials, and activists have all worked together to try to stop the spread of HIV and AIDS in the United States. Today, all blood is screened before it is given to a patient, and doctors do everything they can to stop the transmission of the virus from mothers to their newborn children. Despite all efforts to combat the epidemic, however, the spread of HIV is still very real.

Every year, the Centers for Disease Control and Prevention (CDC) in Atlanta, Georgia, tracks the spread of HIV in the United States. Through December 2001, a total of 807,075 people were reported to have had AIDS in the United States. Of these, 462,653, or 57 percent, were known to have died.[4] Of the total deaths, 5,257, or more than one percent, were among children under the age of fifteen.[5]

By December 2001, 4,428 teenagers were reported to have AIDS. Approximately 2,555, or 58 percent, of these were male and 1,873, or 42 percent, were female.[6]

There were 9,074 cases of AIDS reported in American children under the age of thirteen, including 175 children who were reported to have contracted AIDS during the year 2001 alone. Approximately 8,284 children, or 91 percent of the total 9,074, became infected with HIV because their mothers were HIV-positive. Approximately 236 children, or 3 percent of pediatric AIDS cases, were hemophiliacs, and 381 children, or 4 percent, had been exposed to HIV through contaminated blood products, such as transfusions.[7]

An Epidemic or a War?

More Americans have died as a result of the AIDS epidemic than lost their lives in World War II. Nearly eight times as many died of AIDS as were killed in Vietnam.[8] Some cities have lost more people to AIDS than to World Wars I and II, Korea, and Vietnam combined—San Francisco, in fact, lost four times as many young men.[9] As Robert Klitzman wrote in his book *Being Positive: The Lives of Men and Women with HIV*:

> In war . . . families and governments praise soldiers for fighting, and decorate warriors as heroes. For most soldiers, the threat of death ends at some point, and civilian life resumes. They or their survivors also receive pensions and other benefits for years to come. AIDS provides none of these compensations.[10]

AIDS is indeed very much like a war. As Ana Oliveira, Executive Director of Gay Men's Health Crisis in New York City, wrote:

> Ours is a war with no boundaries, it seems. As a community, we have waged battles valiantly, achieved many hard-won accomplishments— always with the reliance on the power of personal commitment and the change that comes when people of conscience act in the service of what they believe is right.[11]

People who have HIV and AIDS, their friends and

families, classmates and co-workers, and all concerned people around the world—everyone who supports the fight against AIDS—is actually part of one of the biggest wars the world has ever seen. One of the most effective guns in this battle is education. It is necessary to find a way to combat HIV and AIDS

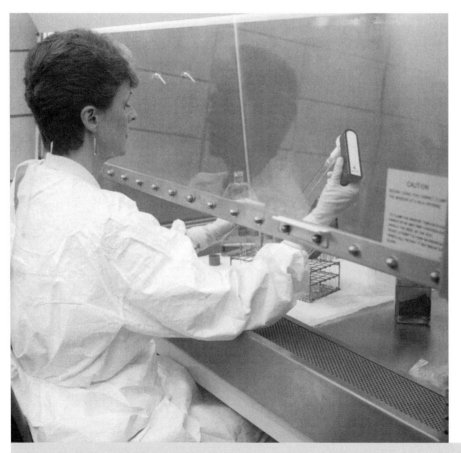

AIDS research led to the development of drugs to combat the disease and prevent the transmission from mother to child. However, there is still no vaccine and no cure.

Spotlight on GMHC

In August 1981, about eighty men gathered in writer Larry Kramer's New York City apartment as news spread about a rare form of cancer that was being found in gay men throughout the city. The cancer was Kaposi's sarcoma, and its emergence announced the birth of a new epidemic, which was eventually called AIDS. Concerned, the men passed a hat around the room to raise money for research about the disease. That night they raised a total of $6,635, and in January 1982, the group named themselves Gay Men's Health Crisis, or GMHC.[12]

GMHC began the world's first AIDS hot line in May 1982, and the hot line received one hundred calls on the first night.[13] The organization grew quickly, and today, GMHC is a respected AIDS service organization, a nonprofit, nongovernmental group that provides services to people with HIV and AIDS. AIDS service organizations are usually charities, and they often receive donations from individuals, foundations, corporations, and government agencies.

GMHC is also considered to be one of the most important HIV/AIDS prevention and care organizations in the world.[14] GMHC offers services such as medical care, counseling, legal assistance, food service, prevention and treatment education, and much more. Each year, GMHC serves more than eleven thousand clients, approximately one-quarter of the people living with HIV and AIDS in New York City.[15] Although the organization was founded to help gay men learn how to protect themselves from AIDS and to help gay men who had HIV and AIDS, today GMHC serves men, women, and children, regardless of their sexual orientation.

for those people who have the disease, but more lives can be saved if people know what AIDS is, what causes it, and how its transmission can be prevented.

AIDS Education After Twenty Years: Successes and Challenges

Ryan White's experience in Kokomo is an example of the kinds of discrimination that may come with ignorance. The people of Kokomo did not understand HIV and AIDS, and they were afraid. The young people in Cicero, however, were offered education about the disease, and because they understood AIDS, they were not afraid of Ryan and welcomed him into their school. They understood that he was just like them in many ways and that he deserved their respect and friendship. As the students learned how AIDS can affect people who have the disease, they also learned how to protect themselves from becoming infected.

Today, because of Ryan White and others who saw the need for AIDS education, most people in the United States know about AIDS and how HIV is transmitted. Young people can learn about HIV and AIDS in their schools and communities, on the Internet, or in books such as this one. Today people in the United States are less afraid to talk about AIDS in general terms than they were fifteen years ago. AIDS is discussed in newspapers and by reporters on television news, and characters with HIV and AIDS have been seen on popular television shows and in movies. The fight against AIDS has been taken up by many groups, including people in the entertainment industry who have helped the cause by using their fame to show their support. However, discrimination and fear are still very common. One woman said:

> For a long time I felt like a big germ—an infected person, tainted, able to infect other people. HIV is like leprosy. Lepers were outcasts, separated from everybody else and thrown together on an island to isolate them. That's how I felt.[16]

It is important to understand HIV and AIDS in order to protect oneself, to fight discrimination, and to provide assistance to those who need it.

Has the Battle Been Won?

AIDS activists have made great strides in educating people in the United States about AIDS. Many Americans are not as afraid to talk about AIDS as they were in the early days of the epidemic, and doctors and activists have worked very hard to make information available to anyone who wants it. These are positive steps, and doctors and activists are finding new ways to educate people all the time.

It is important, however, for people to remember that there are still no cures for HIV and AIDS. Unfortunately, now that information and treatment are readily available, many people in the United States are beginning to think that they do not need to worry about contracting HIV anymore and that it is not a serious health problem. A poll showed that in 1987, 75 percent of Americans considered AIDS to

Showing Support:
Red Ribbons and the AIDS Quilt

The symbol of AIDS awareness is a looped red ribbon. When a person wears a red ribbon, he or she is showing support for people with HIV and AIDS and the fight against the epidemic. Famous people often wear a red ribbon when making public appearances, and their support helps people to understand how HIV and AIDS has affected people from all walks of life, regardless of whether or not they have HIV or AIDS themselves.

Another way people have shown support for those with HIV and AIDS is the AIDS Quilt. The AIDS Quilt was started in 1986 by the NAMES Project. The quilt is made up of panels made by families and friends to honor people who have died of AIDS. The quilts include pictures, pieces of clothing, drawings, and mementos of people who have died. Every year, the quilt travels around the world to promote awareness of HIV and AIDS and to help people learn about the epidemic.

The looped red ribbon has become the universal symbol of AIDS awareness.

be the country's most serious health concern. As people learned more about HIV and AIDS, their fears subsided, and in 1995, only 45 percent of Americans considered AIDS to be the country's most serious health problem. By 2000, that number had dropped to 26 percent.[17]

Although it is necessary for people to understand HIV and AIDS and not be afraid of people who have it, doctors, researchers, and AIDS activists are concerned that people may return to practicing high-risk behavior under the false impression that the fight against HIV and AIDS is over. HIV is a deadly virus, and although there are treatments available today to help people with HIV and AIDS live longer, more productive lives, this does not mean that the disease has been erased from the American landscape. Although Americans are now more ready to talk about AIDS in a general sense, people with HIV and AIDS are often still afraid to disclose their AIDS status, and they still face discrimination in terms of fair and affordable medical treatment, housing, and immigration, among other issues.

5

Advocacy, Roadblocks, and Debates

Organizations such as GMHC have been essential to the fight against the spread of HIV and AIDS, and they are vital support centers for people living with the disease. AIDS service organizations provide prevention education and treatment therapy, and they often work with communities to offer services that local governments cannot or will not provide. Often, AIDS service organizations also help to provide legal services to people living with HIV and AIDS, and they work to combat discrimination in the community. Individuals from these

67

organizations engage in AIDS advocacy, which means that they help to ensure the rights of people with AIDS, and they raise awareness and political support in addition to raising resources for research, prevention, and care.

Many experts contend that the AIDS epidemic has helped the world to change the way it deals with health issues in general because of the active involvement of AIDS activists from the beginning of the epidemic. Activists were often the catalysts behind HIV-prevention campaigns. At times, their public protests have even shaped political decisions. Activists have helped to inform the public about HIV and AIDS, and they helped public and private organizations understand the significance of the epidemic.

In a special section dedicated to "AIDS At 20," Robert Pear of *The New York Times* wrote:

> The AIDS epidemic has profoundly altered the way government responds to health emergencies, galvanizing medical research, speeding the review of drugs and forcing officials who make health policy to share power with patients and their advocates.[1]

Pear explained that the AIDS epidemic has caused patients and politicians to have a very different kind of relationship than they have had in the past. AIDS, for example, caused many politicians to reevaluate their views on such issues as health insurance, substance abuse policies, child care, education, and equal rights for gays and lesbians.

Some AIDS activists have taken part in acts of civil disobedience, which is usually a peaceful form of resistance used to protest the unfairness of laws and decrees. One of the most well-known AIDS activist groups is ACT-UP, the AIDS Coalition to Unleash Power, which was formed in 1987 by a group of people who felt that the U.S. government was mismanaging the AIDS crisis.[2] When Larry Kramer, the founder of GMHC, was forming ACT-UP, he helped people to realize the seriousness of the situation by showing them how much they had to lose by doing nothing. Kramer reportedly told the group of gay men who had met to discuss their plans, "Half of you will be dead in seven years."[3] The grim reality of this statement inspired the group. Today, the organization's slogan is:

AIDS=Genocide
Silence=Death
Fight Back!

ACT-UP has engaged in many acts of civil disobedience in an attempt to change public policy. ACT-UP members have protested by blocking traffic on the Golden Gate Bridge in San Francisco, sitting in during a mass at St. Patrick's Cathedral in New York City, and launching huge protests at the Food and Drug Administration (FDA) headquarters. One of the most famous of the FDA demonstrations was in 1988, when more than one thousand people protested to demand the faster approval of new AIDS therapies. Police arrested more than 170 people during the protest.[4]

Many people believe that they can make a difference by making their opinions understood through activism. They often feel that this is a very effective way of changing government policy or public opinion. David Barr, a lawyer who went to his first ACT-UP meeting in 1987, said:

> I had already been involved in AIDS work, but with ACT-UP, I immediately felt a sense of camaraderie and community that had been missing from the gay community. I was excited by all of the energy and anger, by people coming together for a purpose and a cause.[5]

By working with ACT-UP, Barr felt that he was able to make a difference in the fight against AIDS.

Some activists feel that Americans are becoming complacent, or satisfied with the way things are, about HIV and AIDS. AIDS groups had made significant strides in teaching people about the possible consequences of high-risk behavior. However, many experts now fear that because of this complacency, people are beginning to engage in high-risk activities again, which will cause a resurgence in the epidemic. David Barr, who was diagnosed with HIV in 1989, is concerned that the availability of relatively effective drugs is causing people to engage in high-risk activities, despite efforts to teach the community about ways to prevent the spread of HIV. Barr says:

> Now, even though I feel very fortunate to be alive, I'm worried. So many young gay men don't know the history. They think they can just take a pill and be O.K. But engagement in organizations is down, and infection rates are up, and the AIDS epidemic is nowhere near over in the gay community.[6]

This is the way many people deal with HIV.

A lot of people figure HIV isn't something they have to worry about. It's something other people get, not them. But anyone can get HIV infection if they are sharing drug needles and syringes or having sex with an infected person.

HIV infection can happen to you if you take chances or pretend it doesn't exist.

There are some general rules. Never share drug needles and syringes. And unless you're sure your partner isn't infected, don't take a chance. Or at least use a latex condom, correctly, every time you have sex.

Understand HIV and AIDS. Call the Tennessee AIDS hotline at 1-800-525-AIDS. Call 1-800-243-7889 (TTY) for deaf access.

HIV is the virus that causes AIDS.

TENNESSEE RESPONDS TO AIDS

Tennessee Department of Health and Environment. Authorization No. 343945. (Dec. 1990). 3,800 copies. This public document was promulgated at a cost of 10c per copy.

Public service messages, such as this poster used in Tennessee, urge people to become informed and take action to prevent HIV and AIDS.

Roadblocks to Education

Doctors, researchers, and activists have argued for a long time that one of the best ways to combat the spread of HIV and AIDS is to teach people about the disease and how it is transmitted. Many social and political leaders, however, raised concerns early on in the epidemic about AIDS education because it often means the discussion of topics considered taboo by many, such as sex, homosexuality, and drug use.

Many activists criticize the way the government dealt with the AIDS epidemic during the 1980s. Some argue that the epidemic grew because President Ronald Reagan did not discuss AIDS in an in-depth way until 1987, six years after the epidemic was recognized by the medical community. One of President Reagan's advisers later said that the president was wary of discussing ways to prevent AIDS transmission because he "did not want to get into arguments about the effectiveness of condoms, or whether certain kinds of sex can ever be safe."[7]

Other conservative politicians, such as Senator Jesse Helms, fought to keep educational pamphlets on safer sex from receiving federal funding because they felt that the pamphlets would "encourage or promote homosexual sexual activity."[8] Organizations such as GMHC and the American Civil Liberties Union (ACLU) fought against the ban. In 1992, the organizations finally succeeded in getting a federal court to strike down the restrictions.[9]

Sex Education in Schools

One of the major debates about AIDS education is the issue of sex education in schools. Some people feel that children should not receive sex education classes in school and that it is the parents' responsibility alone to teach children about sex. Some argue that offering sex education and teaching about safer sex in a school setting encourages young people to have sex before they are ready. And some people do not want schools to discuss anal sex because they think that this encourages young people to engage in homosexual sex. Many people believe that any kind of sexual activity outside of marriage is wrong, and some people believe that it is wrong to even talk about sex, in public or in private.

Those who advocate sex education, on the other hand, argue that young people should know about sex in order to make informed decisions about whether or not they want to have sex. While many sex education advocates agree that it is necessary to teach abstinence, or the choice not to have sex, they argue that young people are exposed to sexual issues all the time. They point out that most young people regularly see sex discussed and portrayed in television and movies, and they argue that it is irresponsible not to address these issues in a public forum. They believe that young people need to learn about sex and safer sex practices in order to understand that HIV and other diseases can be transmitted through unprotected oral, anal, and vaginal sex. They claim that young people have a right to know about sex and how to protect themselves from unwanted pregnancy, sexually transmitted diseases, and destructive relationships.

Advocates for sex education usually encourage parents to discuss sex with their children, but they also argue that young people benefit from in-school sex education because children and parents sometimes have trouble discussing sensitive issues such as sex. They argue that if sex education is offered in school, then there is a better chance that all children will be informed about topics they believe to be essential to healthy living. There have been many studies done on the effects of sex education on sexual activity among young people, and none of the studies have proven that sex education increases the sexual activities of students—in fact, several studies have shown the opposite.[10]

Many schools have made sex education a part of the curriculum, but there are often significant and sometimes very vocal public debates regarding the emphasis of the instruction. In May 1986, for example, Surgeon General C. Everett Koop issued a report about AIDS in which he called for AIDS education for children of all ages and advocated the use of condoms to stop the spread of disease.[11] In the report he said, "Education concerning AIDS must start at the lowest grade possible as part of any health and hygiene program."[12] Koop's recommendations were not acted upon, however, and fifteen years later he said that "too many people 'placed conservative ideology far above saving human lives.'"[13]

Although some people object to sex education in schools, many experts believe that teaching young people about AIDS transmission and prevention is a crucial part of stopping the epidemic.

Even discussions about abstinence and alternatives to sexual intercourse have caused controversy. In December 1994, for example, President Clinton fired then U.S. Surgeon General Joycelyn Elders when she said that masturbation "perhaps should be taught" in schools as a safe alternative to intercourse.[14]

Condoms

Studies have proven that when used properly, condoms significantly reduce the risk of HIV transmission. Condoms can be purchased at pharmacies and are available at clinics and in some schools. Latex and polyurethane condoms are much more effective than lambskin condoms in preventing pregnancy and the spread of sexually transmitted diseases, because they help to contain the flow of semen during ejaculation. There are many different kinds of condoms available on the market today, but no condom is 100 percent effective. Condoms may break, and if they are used incorrectly, they may leak.

In 1994, the female condom came on the market, although it had been developed in the 1980s.[15] If used properly, it can be as effective as the male condom in terms of preventing pregnancy and the spread of sexually transmitted diseases because it keeps bodily fluids such as semen from entering the vagina or from coming into contact with the mucous membranes of the vagina. One advantage of female condoms is that they can be inserted many hours before sex, and some women feel that they have more control over their protection when they use female condoms. Like male condoms, female condoms can be purchased at pharmacies without prescription, and they are available in clinics and in some schools. Unfortunately, some people find female condoms to be uncomfortable and difficult to use properly. Because of these problems, female condoms are considered to be less safe and effective than male condoms. They also tend to be more expensive and sometimes harder to find than male condoms.

Should Condoms Be Advertised?

Some people argue that it is inappropriate to advertise condoms or to have public education campaigns encouraging the use of condoms. Some people are offended by condom advertisements or by discussions of condoms on television or in movies. AIDS educators and activists, however, argue that condoms have been proven to reduce the risk of transmission of HIV and other sexually transmitted diseases and that it is therefore necessary to educate the public. They say that the need for education outweighs the risk of offending people.

Advocates argue that if people know what condoms are and where they are available, and if there is less of a stigma attached to their use, then people will be more inclined to protect themselves from HIV and other sexually transmitted diseases by using condoms. Those opposed to public advertising of condoms, however, argue that advertisements for

Though there are those who object to advertising condoms, others believe it is important to educate people about them as a means of preventing AIDS. Shown is a marketplace in Addis Ababa, Ethiopia, with a billboard advertising condoms.

condoms promote sex outside of marriage, thereby contributing to the epidemic by encouraging people to have multiple sex partners. Despite the arguments from AIDS activists, it was not until the mid-1980s that condoms began to be advertised in newspapers and magazines and on television, and even then, it was very rare. Although the arguments are still hotly debated, today condoms are also advertised on subways and buses, in ads during movie previews, and even in bars and restaurants.

Condoms in Schools?

One of the biggest debates about condoms is the question of condom distribution in junior and senior high schools, and the American public is still very much divided over the issue. Although it has not been proven, many people argue that if condoms are available to students free of charge in their schools, then they will be more inclined to have sex. Other people argue that some teenagers are already having sex and that those who are will be more likely to use condoms if they know where to get them and if they are easily available. Although many clinics and hospitals will give free condoms to those who request them and many colleges give away condoms in dormitories, approximately half of Americans believe that teenage students "should receive only information in schools." Less than half of Americans polled believe that teenagers should be able to get condoms in school.[16]

The Need for HIV Testing

One of the main reasons that the AIDS epidemic has spread so quickly and indiscriminately throughout the world is that HIV is a virus that is difficult to recognize right away without a blood test. Many people, for example, have the virus and pass it on to other people before they even feel or look sick. In addition, the virus may lie undetected for several months after the period of infection. This is known as the "window period," and it is one of the reasons that people often need to be tested more than once. Furthermore, the tests can be expensive and hard to find in some parts of the world. Even when the tests are available, many people are afraid of the outcome of the test and therefore refuse to get it done. It is important to note, however, that the monetary costs of getting tested are far lower than the emotional, social, and economic costs of *not* getting tested and furthering the spread of the disease.

In the beginning of the AIDS epidemic, before anyone understood how the disease was transmitted, doctors were at a loss as to how to determine whether a person even had AIDS or not. It was several years before an answer to this mystery was presented, and it required a significant under-standing of the disease. After beginning to understand the virus that causes AIDS, doctors learned that the immune system releases chemicals called antibodies to try to destroy the HIV cells. In 1985, a test was licensed to determine whether or not there were HIV antibodies in a patient's blood. This test greatly helped doctors to combat the spread of the disease, because it allowed them to test people for HIV antibodies and determine the prevalence of infection in the population.

Once these tests were licensed, blood banks across America began to screen the nation's blood supply for the virus that causes AIDS. This in turn helped to significantly decrease the possibility of contracting HIV through contaminated blood products. Today there is hardly any chance of contracting HIV from blood products.

What Is an HIV Test?

An HIV test does not actually detect the virus. The test shows only that there are HIV antibodies in the blood. It does not determine whether or not a person has AIDS or when or if he or she will develop AIDS. A person is considered HIV-positive, or seropositive, if there are HIV antibodies in his or her blood. This usually means that the person has HIV. If a person is HIV-negative, or seronegative, he or she does not have HIV antibodies in his or blood, and this usually means that he or she does not have HIV. A negative test result does not mean that a person will never be infected with HIV, and people should be aware that an HIV-negative test does not mean that they are immune to the virus.

The test most commonly used to determine the presence of HIV antibodies is known as the ELISA test, or the *enzyme-linked immunosorbent assay*, which is done by a machine. ELISA is usually quite accurate, but it is sometimes known to give results that falsely indicate that a person has HIV. This is known as a *false-positive* test. Because health care providers know that the ELISA test may report a false-positive result, blood that tests positive for HIV in an ELISA test is tested again using a test known as the *Western blot test*, which is done by hand. The

The first HIV test was developed and marketed in 1985. Because the virus may not be detected at the beginning of the infection, many people need to be tested more than once. Shown above is a technician filling out diagnosis forms.

Western blot test is a more accurate test, and it often takes a few days to a few weeks to process the results. Usually the Western blot test is accurate, but if the test results are considered inconclusive, then a person should be tested again in a few weeks. If a person tests positive for HIV in an ELISA test and in a Western blot test, then it can be assumed that he or she is HIV-positive.

Testing for HIV antibodies is usually an effective means of determining a person's HIV status. There are some exceptions, however. Children who have been born to HIV-positive mothers usually carry some of the mothers' antibodies in their blood for the first six to eighteen months. They do not always carry the virus, and they may never get AIDS. It is also important to note that the body does not begin to make HIV antibodies right away. There may be a delay of several months before the body begins to manufacture HIV antibodies in earnest. Thus, if a person has only recently been infected with HIV, the HIV antibody test may not be accurate during this window period. Doctors suggest that six months is a reasonable amount of time to wait before being sure that a negative test result is accurate.

Anonymous Testing

Many people choose to go to a special clinic to be tested for HIV, and people often prefer to be tested for the virus only if they can remain anonymous. The Food and Drug Administration approved a home HIV testing kit in 1996, which has helped some people feel more comfortable about getting tested.

There are several reasons why many people prefer to be tested anonymously. For example, many people have been discriminated against after testing positive for HIV. They have lost their jobs and their homes. Some have faced fear, anger, confusion, and even violence from people who learn that they have HIV. Legal prosecution against people with HIV and AIDS is common in much of the world, and one recent study showed that protecting the human rights of people with HIV "remains a low priority for much of the world's lawmakers."[17] Some countries around the world have even taken measures to keep people with HIV from living in society. The study showed that eleven of the countries surveyed, or 25 percent of the world's population, had laws that required forced quarantine of people with HIV, even though this is a practice that is discouraged by much of the world health community.[18]

Legal Issues

In the United States, people with HIV and AIDS are protected by a wide variety of laws. The Americans with Disabilities Act (ADA), for example, is an important law that protects people with disabilities by guaranteeing them equal opportunities and prohibiting discrimination. The ADA protects people with HIV and AIDS as well as their family, friends, and caretakers.[19]

Mandatory testing for HIV is the subject of heated debate. In the United States, testing for HIV is usually voluntary, but there are some organizations that require mandatory HIV testing, including government organizations such as the Peace Corps, the Job Corps, the Foreign Service, the National Guard, and the armed services. Applicants for the Peace Corps and the Foreign Service will be rejected if they test positive, and military personnel will be discharged. Mandatory testing is becoming common in prisons in the United States and in the rest of the world.

Although many people feel that their right to privacy outweighs the government's right to know their HIV status, governments around the world contend that tracking the spread of HIV is necessary to help fight the epidemic. The CDC issues surveillance reports documenting the number of new AIDS cases each year. It relies on reports from all states regarding new cases of AIDS, although as of December 2001, only thirty-five states, the U.S. Virgin Islands, and Guam reported new cases of HIV in addition to the numbers of new cases of AIDS.[20]

One debate about mandatory HIV testing concerns the testing of pregnant women and newborns. Some people argue that it is necessary to test all pregnant women and newborns in order to track cases of HIV and AIDS in women and to determine the spread of HIV in the general population. Some also argue that all pregnant women should be tested so that those who are HIV-positive can be given drugs to reduce the transmission of the virus to the baby. Between 1988 and 1995, the CDC conducted a program to test newborns for HIV in forty-five states, although the test results were kept anonymous. The results of this test helped the CDC track the spread of the epidemic.[21] Mandatory testing of pregnant women and newborns is a highly controversial issue, however, and many opponents argue that it is, at best, ineffective without a guarantee that women and infants who test positive will receive adequate medical treatment. This is of particular importance in countries where care for HIV and AIDS is difficult to obtain.

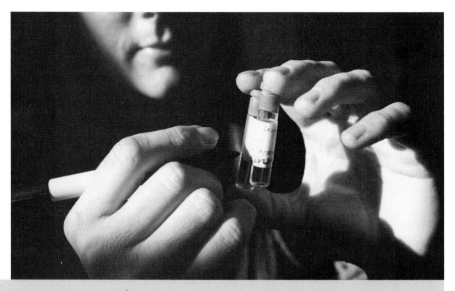

Many people prefer to be tested for HIV anonymously. In the United States, while most testing is voluntary, some organizations—such as the military and the Peace Corps—require that applicants be tested.

Immigration and Travel

People with HIV or AIDS may encounter difficulties when traveling, but not just because their health is poor. Many nations have restrictions that keep people with HIV or AIDS from entering the country, and this is a serious concern for AIDS advocates.

Some health officials in these countries, including some officials in the United States, have argued that because HIV is a contagious disease, people with HIV or AIDS are a possible health risk and should therefore not be allowed the same rights of travel as other people as a matter of national security. Some believe that people with HIV or AIDS should not be allowed to obtain travel visas or to have certain immigration rights because they may engage in risky behavior and transmit the disease without the knowledge of people in the host country. Some countries require HIV tests before they grant visas to travelers. Other countries allow for the possibility of testing people who are suspected of being HIV-positive or refusing entry to people suspected of engaging in high-risk behavior. Other countries may exclude travelers who have declared their HIV-positive status.

Advocates for people with HIV and AIDS argue that travel restrictions violate the human rights of people with the disease. The issue of travel restrictions for people with HIV and AIDS is a major topic of debate in the United States because these restrictions have the power to affect immigration, the opportunities for infected persons to attend conferences or visit doctors in the United States, and much more. The United States has several laws restricting immigration and travel for people with HIV, and many people involved in the fight against AIDS have opposed these laws. In 1992, for example, Harvard University moved the 7th Annual International Conference on AIDS to Amsterdam, Holland, to protest policies barring people with HIV and AIDS from entering the United States.

Drugs and Drug Availability

There are many drugs available today that help people with HIV. Antiretroviral drugs help the immune system stay strong by stopping the virus from reproducing in the blood. In addition, there are many different kinds of drugs that treat the opportunistic infections common to people with HIV and AIDS. When treating patients with HIV and AIDS, doctors usually prescribe a drug cocktail, or a combination of medication consisting of at least three different kinds of drugs, which helps to stabilize or lower the body's *viral load*, or the amount of HIV in the blood. Some common antiretroviral drugs include AZT, the first AIDS drug approved by the Food and Drug Administration, ddI, and ddC. Drug cocktails often include some combination of drugs like these with a protease inhibitor, which targets a different part of the HIV reproduction process.

Unfortunately, drugs used to combat HIV and AIDS are often very toxic, and there are sometimes serious side effects. In addition, people with HIV and AIDS often find that they are faced with a serious regimen of pill-taking that may be difficult to stick to, since it is sometimes necessary to take several different drugs at different times of the day. Drugs also affect people in different ways, and antiretroviral drugs often become less effective over time as the body builds up a tolerance to them. When this happens, people with HIV and AIDS must change their drug cocktail to something that works better. Some AIDS service organizations provide services to people with HIV and AIDS to help them keep up with difficult drug treatment regimens.

There are many points of debate about AIDS drug therapy. Because AIDS medications are often difficult to administer, people with HIV and AIDS must be educated about the available drugs and treatment options. Opportunities for treatment are developing very rapidly, and it is very challenging for people to keep up with shifting medical developments. People with HIV are advised to see an HIV/AIDS specialist when they are diagnosed with the disease, because specialists are more likely to know of the new opportunities for treatment. People with HIV and AIDS must also visit their doctors frequently to make sure that their medications are working properly. This can become quite costly, and adequate medical insurance is necessary in order to ensure proper treatment. In the United States, there are several laws that can help people with HIV and AIDS get the treatment and drug therapies they need. In addition to helping people with HIV and AIDS to cope with the disease, many service organizations have specialists devoted to helping people make their way through the legal mazes that sometimes keep people from getting the medical attention they need.

Treatment in the Global Arena

Unfortunately, in many parts of the world, it is nearly impossible to get adequate treatment for HIV and AIDS, even if there are systems in place to educate people about the disease and how it is spread. Sometimes the cost of antiretroviral drugs exceeds the average wage by such a high amount that only the very rich can afford them. To make matters worse, some countries are unable, or unwilling, to make antiretroviral drugs available through public medical programs. Some countries, such as Brazil, have made huge strides in fighting the epidemic by overhauling faltering health systems.[22] Drug companies have argued that it is impossible for them to simply give away the drugs to developing countries without raising the costs in other parts of the world. Many companies have also fought to keep the patents for their drugs away from other companies who might make generic versions of them.

The high cost of HIV and AIDS drugs is only part of the issue, however. Even if pharmaceutical companies were to donate all the drugs that are necessary, there would still be huge obstacles to effective drug treatment in some areas of the world. In many parts of the world, such as in sub-Saharan Africa, there is not adequate refrigeration for medication, nor are there good roads on which to transport the drugs to those who need them. AIDS drugs also require such strict medical supervision that it is necessary for trained health professionals to assist those using the drugs. If there is no one trained to administer the antiretroviral medications, then the drugs could be used incorrectly, and this in itself could be deadly. In addition to training for the administration of these powerful drugs, health professionals need special tools with which to test their patients' immune systems. These tests are often expensive and difficult to use because laboratories are too far away.[23]

Many doctors in the developing world argue that a fair distribution of drugs is essential to the fight against the AIDS epidemic. On the other hand, some also argue that prevention and education are more important. Many doctors argue that it is essential to fight HIV and AIDS but that it is also necessary for people to have clean water and nourishing food—and many parts of the world face serious health problems due to the lack of food and water. The AIDS epidemic has only made conditions in these countries worse. In these situations, antiretroviral drugs are actually a kind of nightmare to some doctors. Suniti Solomon, a doctor who treated the first AIDS cases in India, is one doctor who is concerned that improper drug treatment will actually make the epidemic worse. She said, "Drugs used the wrong way kill people—and they are used the wrong way all the time. We have to get more training. Food. Clean water. Give us condoms, for God's sake. Teach women to read. But keep your drugs. They really won't help us now."[24]

6

AIDS in the New Millennium

Vaccines are very powerful tools used by doctors around the world. In the United States, for example, infants are vaccinated for a wide array of diseases, and this has helped to stop such diseases as polio and the measles. Vaccines have even helped to rid the world of some diseases completely, such as smallpox, which was eradicated completely by the late 1970s after the World Health Organization launched a worldwide vaccination campaign against the disease in 1967. A vaccine for HIV would be a powerful weapon in the fight against AIDS, but it is proving to be a very

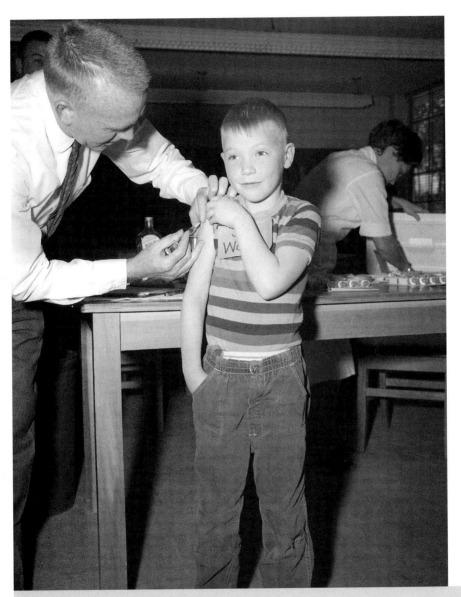

Shown above is a boy receiving a shot for measles as part of a vaccination campaign in 1962. It is hoped that one day a vaccine to prevent AIDS will also be developed.

difficult weapon to make. To date, there is no proven HIV vaccine, although researchers have tested at least thirty potential vaccines since 1987.[1]

When a person contracts a disease like the chicken pox, he or she is unlikely to get the chicken pox again, because the body has built up an immunity to the disease. An immunity is built up when the immune system creates antibodies to fight off an infection that has entered the body. A vaccine is made up of killed or weakened bacteria or virus cells, and it is a kind of defense mechanism for the immune system. Usually a vaccine is given to a patient by an injection, but vaccines are sometimes taken by mouth. A vaccine works by causing the immune system to form antibodies to fight off the bacteria or virus *before* the body is exposed to the real disease. This means that the body becomes immune to the disease without ever having had it.

Unfortunately, as Dr. Luc Montagnier, one of the codiscoverers of HIV, has said, "Vaccine, a magic word, is still a dream for AIDS researchers."[2] HIV attacks cells in the immune system itself, making it very difficult for doctors and researchers to discover ways to help the immune system fight back. There are several approaches that researchers are hoping will lead to a successful vaccine, but it is unlikely that any will be on the market within the decade.[3] Most of the vaccines in progress involve taking harmless parts of HIV and injecting them into cells in the hopes that the cells will then form antibodies that can block infection. People who volunteer to test AIDS vaccines should note that the vaccine may cause them to test HIV-positive even though there is no risk of HIV infection from the vaccine itself. People involved in vaccine trials may also be part of a *control group*, which means that instead of the possible vaccine, they will receive a placebo (a substance containing no medication). There are many health concerns involved with vaccine testing, and people are advised to talk to their doctors before volunteering for any drug trials.

How to Help

Young people can be key players in the fight against AIDS. The first step is to become informed about

The NAMES Project AIDS quilt, shown on display in front of the Washington Monument, consists of panels made by families and friends to honor those who have died of AIDS.

AIDS and HIV and about the issues surrounding the epidemic. There are many books available, and newspapers and magazines report medical advancements and policy changes. The Internet is a very valuable tool when learning about HIV and AIDS, especially since developments are very rapid. It is necessary, however, to know one's sources when using the Internet. Out-of-date information can be very misleading, and one should always confirm the accuracy of information found online.

Young people can also get involved in the fight against AIDS by volunteering for their local AIDS service organizations or by taking part in fund-raisers for AIDS research. Many schools and community centers offer activities that help to build AIDS awareness, and most of these organizations encourage participation of people of all ages.

A Future Without AIDS?

When asked what it has been like fighting AIDS for twenty years, doctors are often at a loss for words. One doctor says the following about her career taking care of people with HIV and AIDS:

> It's like running up a long, slow hill for miles, and then finally the ground begins to level off. It's like waiting for the subway forever, when suddenly the tiny glow of headlights comes ricocheting off the walls ahead. It's like joining the Marines, joining the circus and taking up holy orders, all on the same day.[4]

The AIDS epidemic has challenged the world for over twenty years now, and although much has been achieved, there are still many questions left unanswered. Although there may be a light at the end of the tunnel, the end of the tunnel is still a very long way off, and much needs to be done. People of all ages must be educated. Steps must be taken to help prevent the spread of the disease and to alleviate the societal pressures that encourage people to engage in high-risk behaviors. Antiretroviral drugs must be made more affordable and more available, and people need to be trained in the safe administration of these drugs. A vaccine must be developed, tested successfully, and then distributed worldwide. These are just some of the efforts that must be made before the world can control—and perhaps, someday, end—this terrifying epidemic.

Chapter Notes

Chapter 1. The AIDS Epidemic

1. Linda Villarosa, "One Disease, Lived Six Different Ways," *The New York Times*, June 5, 2001, p. F6.

2. Ibid.

3. Joint United Nations Programme on HIV/AIDS (UNAIDS) and World Health Organization, "AIDS Epidemic Update: December 2002," 2002, p. 3.

4. Ibid., p. 4.

5. Centers for Disease Control and Prevention, "CDC Update: A Glance at the HIV Epidemic," December 2002, <www.cdc.gov/nchstp/od/news/At-a-Glance.pdf> (December 20, 2002).

6. GMHC AIDS Walk New York 2001 brochure.

7. Centers for Disease Control and Prevention.

Chapter 2: The Epidemic and the Spread of AIDS Today

1. Sarah Barbara Watstein with Karen Chandler, *The AIDS Dictionary* (New York: Facts on File, 1998), p. 154.

2. Paul Harding Douglas and Laura Pinsky, The Essential AIDS Fact Book (New York: Pocket Books, 1996), p. 5.

3. Robert Klitzman, *Being Positive: The Lives of Men and Women with HIV* (Chicago: Ivan R. Dee, 1997), p. 41.

4. Watstein, p. 3.

5. Luc Montagnier, *Virus: The Co-Discoverer of HIV Tracks Its Rampage and Charts the Future*, trans. by Stephen Sartarelli (New York: W. W. Norton & Co., 2000), p. 45.

6. Centers for Disease Control and Prevention. *HIV/AIDS Surveillance Report*, 2000, vol. 12, no. 2, p. 1.

7. Douglas and Pinsky, p. 9.

8. Joint United Nations Programme on HIV/AIDS (UNAIDS) and World Health Organization, "AIDS Epidemic Update: December 2002," 2002, p. 6.

9. Douglas and Pinsky, pp. 29–31; Watstein, p. 199.
10. Douglas and Pinsky, p. 14.
11. Ibid., p. 15.
12. Darryl S. Inaba, William E. Cohen, and Michael E. Holstein, *Uppers, Downers, All Arounders: Physical and Mental Effects of Psychoactive Drugs*, 3rd edition (Ashland, Ore.: CNS Publications, Inc., 1997), p. 315.
13. "AIDS Researcher: Man of Year." *Associated Press*, December 21, 1996, <http://www.aegis.com/news/ap/1996/ap961224.html> (January 23, 2002).
14. Klitzman, p. 77.

Chapter 3. A Global Issue

1. Joint United Nations Programme on HIV/AIDS (UNAIDS) and World Health Organization, "AIDS Epidemic Update: December 2002," 2002, pp. 3, 36.
2. Ibid.
3. Ibid., p. 35.
4. Tina Rosenberg, "How to Solve the World's AIDS Crisis: Look at Brazil," *The New York Times Magazine*, January 28, 2001, p. 26.
5. Luc Montagnier, *Virus: The Co-Discoverer of HIV Tracks Its Rampage and Charts the Future*, trans. by Stephen Sartarelli (New York: W. W. Norton & Co., 2000), p. 219.
6. Joint United Nations Programme on HIV/AIDS (UNAIDS) and World Health Organization, 2002, pp. 16, 36.
7. C. Claiborne Ray, "AIDS in Africa," *The New York Times*, June 5, 2001, p. F2; Michael Specter, "India's Plague: Cheaper drugs may help millions who have AIDS— but how many will they hurt?" *The New Yorker*, December 17, 2001, pp. 79–80.
8. Joint United Nations Programme on HIV/AIDS (UNAIDS) and World Health Organization, "AIDS Epidemic Update: December 2001," 2001, p. 18.
9. Donald G. McNeil, Jr., "A Lonely Crusade Warning Africans of AIDS," *The New York Times*, November 28, 2001, p. A1.
10. Donald G. McNiel, Jr., "AIDS and Death Hold No

Sting for Fatalistic Men at African Bar," *The New York Times*, November 29, 2001, p. A14.

11. Joint United Nations Programme on HIV/AIDS (UNAIDS) and World Health Organization, 2002, p. 18.

12. Joint United Nations Programme on HIV/AIDS (UNAIDS) and World Health Organization, 2001, p. 17.

13. Donald G. McNiel, Jr., "AIDS and Death Hold No Sting for Fatalistic Men at African Bar."

14. "Heads in the sand," *The Economist*, September 29, 2001, p. 51.

15. Rosenberg, p. 31.

16. "Deadly meddling," *The Economist*, November 3, 2001, p. 82.

17. Ibid., p. 83.

18. "South Africa: AIDS Drug Trial," *The New York Times*, January 30, 2002, p. A6.

19. "Bush proposes spending $500 million on AIDS," *The New York Times*, June 19, 2002.

20. U.S. Agency for International Development, "The State of the Union: Emergency Plan for AIDS Relief," January 31, 2003, <www.usaid.gov/about/hivaids/excerpts.html> (February 19, 2003).

21. Lawrence K. Altman, "Report, Reversing Estimates, Forecasts Big Increase in AIDS Death Toll," *The New York Times*, July 3, 2002, p. A16; Joint United Nations Programme on HIV/AIDS (UNAIDS) and World Health Organization, 2002, p. 18.

22. Donald G. McNiel, Jr., "AIDS Crisis Leaves Africa's Oldest Ways at a Loss," *The New York Times*, November 27, 2001, p. A8.

23. Joint United Nations Programme on HIV/AIDS (UNAIDS) and World Health Organization, 2001, p. 8.

24. Joint United Nations Programme on HIV/AIDS (UNAIDS) and World Health Organization, 2002, p. 22.

25. Ibid., p. 12.

26. Douglas Frantz, "Drug Use Begetting AIDS in Central Asia," *The New York Times*, August 5, 2001, p. 8.

27. Joint United Nations Programme on HIV/AIDS

(UNAIDS) and World Health Organization, 2001, pp. 10–12.

28. Joint United Nations Programme on HIV/AIDS (UNAIDS) and World Health Organization, 2002, p. 6.

29. Ibid., pp. 6, 7.

30. Montagnier, p. 223.

31. Joint United Nations Programme on HIV/AIDS (UNAIDS) and World Health Organization, 2001, p. 14.

32. Ibid., p. 15.

33. Joint United Nations Programme on HIV/AIDS (UNAIDS) and World Health Organization, 2002, p. 19.

34. Montagnier, p. 45.

35. Rosenberg, p. 28.

Chapter 4. Education and Awareness: Ryan White's Story

1. Ryan White and Ann Marie Cunningham, *Ryan White: My Own Story* (New York: Penguin, 1991), pp. 69–71.

2. Ibid., p. 94.

3. Ibid., p. 175.

4. Centers for Disease Control and Prevention, *HIV/AIDS Surveillance Report*, 2001, vol.13, no. 2, p. 6.

5. Ibid.

6. Ibid., p. 16.

7. Ibid., p. 24.

8. GMHC AIDS Walk New York 2001 brochure.

9. Robert Klitzman, *Being Positive: The Lives of Men and Women with HIV* (Chicago: Ivan R. Dee, 1997), p. 77.

10. Ibid.

11. GMHC AIDS Walk New York 2001 brochure.

12. "At a Glance: Departments and Mission," *Gay Men's Health Crisis Page*, n.d., <http://www.gmhc.org/aboutus/gmhc.html> (January 23, 2002).

13. Ibid.

14. Sarah Barbara Watstein with Karen Chandler, *The AIDS Dictionary* (New York: Facts on File, 1998), p. 108.

15. "At a Glance: Departments and Mission"; GMHC AIDS Walk New York 2001 brochure.

16. Letter from Ana Oliveira, Executive Director, GMHC, June 5, 2001.

17. Klitzman, p. 48.

18. Jayson Blair, "Healthy Skepticism and The Marketing of AIDS," *The New York Times*, August 5, 2001, Section 4, p.14.

Chapter 5. Advocacy, Roadblocks, and Debates

1. Robert Pear, "Advocates for Patients Barged In, and the Federal Government Changed," *The New York Times*, June 5, 2001, p. F3.

2. Sarah Barbara Watstein with Karen Chandler, *The AIDS Dictionary* (New York: Facts on File, 1998), pp. 8–9.

3. Robert Klitzman, *Being Positive: The Lives of Men and Women with HIV* (Chicago: Ivan R. Dee, 1997), p. 233.

4. Pear.

5. Linda Villarosa, "One Disease, Lived Six Different Ways," *The New York Times*, June 5, 2001, p. F6.

6. Ibid.

7. Pear.

8. "At a Glance: Departments and Mission," *Gay Men's Health Crisis Page*, n.d., <www.gmhc.org/aboutus/gmhc.html> (January 23, 2002).

9. Ibid.

10. "Issues and Answers: Fact Sheet on Sexuality Education," Sexuality Information and Education Council of the United States, 2001, <http://www.siecus.org/fact/fact0007.html> (December 17, 2002).

11. "At a Glance: Departments and Mission."

12. Department of Health and Human Services, Public Health Service, *Surgeon General's Report on Acquired Immune Deficiency Syndrome* (Washington, D.C.: Department of Health and Human Services, 1987), p. 4.

13. Pear.

14. "At a Glance: Departments and Mission."

15. Paul Harding Douglas and Laura Pinsky, *The Essential AIDS Fact Book* (New York: Pocket Books, 1996), p. 33.

16. William A. Check, *The Encyclopedia of Health: AIDS* (Philadelphia: Chelsea House Publishers, 1999), pp. 85–86.

17. David Veazey, "Human rights for people with HIV a 'low priority' for world lawmakers," October 26, 2001, <www.reutershealth.com> (October 26, 2001).

18. Ibid.

19. Sarah Barbara Watstein with Karen Chandler, *The AIDS Dictionary* (New York: Facts on File, 1998), p. 14.

20. Centers for Disease Control and Prevention, *HIV/AIDS Surveillance Report*, 2001, vol. 13, no. 2, p. 9, <www.cdc.gov/hiv/stats/nasr1302/table3.htm> (November 26, 2002).

21. Check, p. 38.

22. Tina Rosenberg, "How to Solve the World's AIDS Crisis: Look at Brazil," *The New York Times Magazine*, January 28, 2001, p. 26.

23. Bob Huff, "Low Cost Diagnostics," *GMHC: Treatment Issues*, vol. 15, no. 11/12, November/December 2001, <http://www.gmhc.org/living/treatment/ti15112/ti15112.html> (January 22, 2002).

24. Michael Specter, "India's Plague: Cheaper drugs may help millions who have AIDS —but how many will they hurt?" *The New Yorker*, December 17, 2001, p. 82.

Chapter 6. AIDS in the New Millennium

1. "AIDS vaccines on trial," *The Economist*, February 3, 2001, p. 82.

2. Luc Montagnier, *Virus: The Co-Discoverer of HIV Tracks Its Rampage and Charts the Future*, trans. by Stephen Sartarelli (New York: W. W. Norton & Co., 2000), p. 10.

3. Denise Grady, "Scientists Shifting Strategies in Quest for an AIDS Vaccine," The New York Times, June 5, 2001, p. F1; "Puncturing AIDS," *The Economist*, February 3, 2001, pp. 81–82.

4. Abigail Zuger, "AIDS Doctor Looks Back on a Long, Slow Climb," *The New York Times*, June 5, 2001, p. F1.

Glossary

abstinence—The act of not doing something, such as choosing not to have sex or drink alcohol.

activist—A person who works to achieve a political or social goal through direct action.

AIDS—Acquired immunodeficiency syndrome, a group of diseases that results from a failure of the immune system.

AIDS advocacy—Actions that work to ensure the rights of people with AIDS by promoting awareness and political support in addition to raising resources for research, prevention, and care.

AIDS service organization—An organization that promotes AIDS advocacy, prevention, education, and treatment therapy while providing basic services to people with HIV and AIDS.

antibodies—Chemicals developed by the immune system that work to combat infection.

antiretroviral drug—A drug that fights a retrovirus, or a virus that affects a body's genetic makeup. AZT is a kind of antiretroviral drug.

AZT—Azidothymidine. This was the first and most common drug used to combat HIV. It is made of a material that is similar to a material in human DNA, and thus it helps to keep the HIV retrovirus from attacking a body's DNA.

blood serum—The part of the blood that is clear and separated from anything solid.

CDC—Centers for Disease Control and Prevention. This is a federal agency that works to prevent, control, research, and track diseases, including HIV/AIDS.

civil disobedience—A peaceful form of resistance used to protest the unfairness of laws and decrees.

condom—A latex, polyurethane, or lambskin sheath that is put over the penis while engaging in sexual activity. The "female condom" is a protective latex or polyurethane sheath that fits into a woman's vagina during intercourse.

drug cocktail—Combination of medications consisting of at least three different kinds of drugs that help to stabilize or lower the body's viral load, or the amount of HIV in the blood.

ELISA—Enzyme-linked immunosorbent assay, a test done by a machine that is used to determine the presence of HIV antibodies in a person's body.

GRID—Gay-related immune disease. This was one of the first names for the virus now known as HIV. It was called GRID, or gay cancer, because it seemed to only infect gay men. Doctors and researchers soon realized that this name was inaccurate.

HIV—Human immunodeficiency virus, a virus that affects the immune system in humans and causes AIDS.

immunodeficiency—A defect or a problem with the body's immune system, which is the system in the body that fights off illness and helps people get better when they are sick.

immunosuppression—A state in which the immune system has been interfered with, disturbed, or suppressed.

KS—Kaposi's sarcoma. A cancer of the walls of blood

and lymphatic vessels, characterized by painless purplish blotches on the skin.

opportunistic infections—Infections that healthy bodies would usually be able to fight off but that cause a person with HIV to become very sick.

PCP—*Pneumocystis carinii* pneumonia, a kind of pneumonia that is very rare in people with healthy immune systems. It was one of the first indicators of the AIDS epidemic, and it is one of the leading causes of death in people with AIDS.

protease inhibitor—A kind of drug that blocks the HIV reproductive process by targeting the protease enzyme of the virus. A drug cocktail usually includes a protease inhibitor in combination with a drug like AZT that combats a different part of the virus.

retrovirus—A kind of virus that attacks a body's genetic material.

seronegative—In relationship to HIV/AIDS, this indicates that a person does not have HIV antibodies in his or her blood and is therefore HIV-negative, or not infected with the virus.

seropositive—In relationship to HIV/AIDS, this indicates that a person does have HIV antibodies in his or her blood and is therefore HIV-positive. This means that the person does have HIV and may develop AIDS.

T-helper cell—A kind of white blood cell that the body needs to have a healthy immune system. These cells are also known as CD4 cells or T4 cells.

vaccine—A preventive medicine that is made up of destroyed or weakened bacteria or virus cells. A vaccine works by causing the immune system to form antibodies to fight off the bacteria or virus before the body is exposed to the real disease.

viral load—The amount of HIV in the blood. Doctors often use the viral load to determine how advanced the virus is in a person's body.

Western blot test—A test done by hand to determine the existence of HIV antibodies in a person. A Western blot test is usually very accurate and is often used to determine the accuracy of an ELISA test.

window period—The period between the time when a person becomes infected with HIV and the time when he or she develops HIV antibodies. People can pass HIV on to others during the window period without even knowing it. This period may be from several weeks to several months, and so doctors suggest that a person wait up to six months before accepting an HIV-negative test result.

For More Information

American Institute for Teen AIDS Prevention
PO Box 395
Oberlin, Ohio 77074
817-237-0230

Centers for Disease Control and Prevention
1600 Clifton Road
Atlanta, Ga. 30333
800-311-3435

Elizabeth Glaser Pediatric AIDS Foundation
1730 Rhode Island Ave., NW, Suite 400
Washington, D.C. 20036
888-499-HOPE (4673)

Gay Men's Health Crisis (GMHC)
119 W. 24th Street
New York, N.Y. 10011
212-367-1000

National AIDS Hotline: 800-342-2437
In Spanish: 800-344-7432

National Minority AIDS Council (NMAC)
1931 13th St., NW
Washington, D.C. 20009
202-483-6622

The AIDS Memorial Quilt
PO Box 5552
Atlanta, Ga. 31107
404-688-5500

Further Reading

Books

Brimner, Larry Dane. *The Names Project: The AIDS Quilt*. Danbury, Conn.: Children's Press, 2000.

Gedatus, Gustav Mark. *HIV and AIDS*. Mankato, Minn.: Capstone Press, 2000.

McPhee, Andrew T. *AIDS*. Danbury, Conn.: Franklin Watts, 2000.

Packer, Kenneth L. *HIV Infection: The Facts You Need to Know*. Danbury, Conn.: Franklin Watts, 1998.

Starr, Robert, ed. *AIDS: Why Should I Care? Teens Across America Speak Out*. West Hollywood, Calif.: People Taking Action Against AIDS Press, 1999.

Internet Addresses

American Foundation for AIDS Research (AMFAR)
<http://www.amfar.org>

Centers for Disease Control and Prevention
<http://www.cdc.gov>

Joint United Nations Programme on HIV/AIDS (UNAIDS)
<http://www.unaids.org>

Index

A

Aaron Diamond AIDS
Research Center, 31
abstinence, 73, 76
acquired immunodeficiency
syndrome. See AIDS
African epidemic
AIDS awareness and sex
education, 39–40, 42
availability of medica-
tions, 43–46, 90
causes of, 38–39
crisis level of, 34,
36–38
fight against HIV and
AIDS, 47, 49
government involvement
in, 42–43
progress in drug distrib-
ution, 45
AIDS (acquired
immunodeficiency
syndrome)
causes of, 18–20
epidemic and spread of,
7–12, 13–15,
17–18, 31–32
future without, 96–97
a gender-neutral disease,
23–24
legal issues of, 84–87
worldwide issues of,
33–40, 42–47,
49–53, 89–91
AIDS activists, 63, 64,
65, 66, 67–70, 72,
77–78

AIDS advocacy, 68
AIDS awareness and
education
condoms in school, 79
fight against AIDS,
60–66, 95–97
importance of, 11–12,
58
La Toya Rodgers's story,
5–7
roadblocks to, 72
Ryan White's story,
54–58
sex education in schools,
73–74, 76
AIDS Coalition to Unleash
Power (ACT-UP), 69–70
AIDS quilt, 65
AIDS-related deaths, 34
AIDS service organizations,
67, 68, 88, 89, 96
American Civil Liberties
Union (ACLU), 72
Americans with Disabilities
Act (ADA), 84
anonymous testing, 83–84
antibodies, 19, 30, 80,
82–83
antiretroviral drugs,
43–45, 88, 90, 91, 97
Asia, 49, 50–51
AZT (azidothymidine), 43,
88

B

Barr, David, 70
blood donation, 27
blood serum, 19